Beneath the Lode of the Cross

Reflections on a Journey

Rick Gray

GrayceBook Publishing

8980 Palos Verde Dr.

Orlando, FL 32825

www.GrayceBook.com

E-mail: Grayrick1@gmail.com

ISBN: 978-1983314056

Printed in the United States of America

Acknowledgments

This work is dedicated to Dr. William E. Pannell, friend and mentor. To my wife, Coral, and to all who have been used of God to move me along in this journey to find God's treasure trove, my deepest thanks, some debts can never be repaid.

Wherewithal shall a young man cleanse his way? By taking heed thereto according to thy word.

Thy word have I hid in mine heart, that I might not sin against thee.

Psalms 119: 9,11

Contents

A More Wesleyan Understanding
The Gift of God

Epilogue
Notes
Recommended Resources

"My mind flashed back to a scene a number of years earlier when I lowered her into a tub of water to baptize her into the faith"

Introduction

"Jesus Christ." His name wasn't said in praise, it was being used as an expletive. That realization sent a shiver through me. It had been a long time since I'd been around anyone who would use the Lord's name in vain like that and even more shocking to me was the fact that it had come from the mouth of one so close to me. Immediately, my mind flashed back to a scene a number of years earlier when I lowered her into a tub of water to baptize her into the faith. It was a holy moment and I was sure that its power would forever remain a part of her life's experiences.

Before the baptism, we had talked about the significance of her profession of faith and of the significance of the baptism act. I was sure that she understood but in the reality of the present moment, I realized that my work with her had been incomplete. She didn't understand who Jesus is and why, in our family, his name is never to be used as a cuss word. In the sure belief that that understanding will come, we will talk again. And in case questions should arise after I have been taken from her to be with the Lord, this manuscript will serve as a reminder and as my legacy to her of a personal encounter and faith walk with Jesus Christ that has reshaped my life and ability to give and receive love.

Why am I here?

I was fifteen years old when I was introduced to God's great treasure for me, Jesus Christ. I had spent my early years like so many other young African Americans growing up in the United States, confused, frustrated, angry and alone. Life during the 50s and early 60s had taught me that all the world but me was white and I didn't belong. It was from that sense of alienation that I resigned myself to life and relationships. Life had no meaning or purpose and all my relationships were superficial. It wasn't that I was a closed person who shut everyone out; I just didn't know anyone who wanted to come in. Everyone around me looked like me and, like me, struggled to make sense of his or her place in life. You can imagine my surprise then, when someone sat down with me and shared that God loved me and wanted a personal relationship. I came to learn that he loved me so much that he parted the heavens to become a human being, lived on earth and eventually was killed by the very people he came to love. I was stunned to discover that I shared in his death even though it occurred two thousand years before my birth. I helped to kill Jesus. Not by any deliberate action but by the way that I was internally.

A Voice in the Dark

Life often is very difficult. Many forces seem to be at work persuading people to try various competing courses of action. The focus of those forces is often the young and inexperienced who only understand them to be puzzling and confusing. I spent much of my early life just trying to figure out why I existed. Life was a puzzle I couldn't figure out.

As a young boy, I grew up part of a poor black family in Northwestern Pennsylvania. By all accounts I was a good kid. I was sensitive and had a reputation for being innocent and even nice. I shared my home with a father, a mother and eight siblings. With so many in the small rundown house, it was to be expected that I would share a bedroom with three brothers.

The bedroom was unremarkable, except that the only source of light was a single light bulb in the middle of the ceiling. A long string hung from the chain on the side of the fixture and it had to be yanked in order to turn the light on or off. Also the room was usually a mess. Four boys can accumulate a lot of junk and most of it ended up strewn throughout the room. The bed we all shared, floors and dressers were always covered with mysterious piles. Traveling in the room in the light was only for the brave of heart. To attempt it in the dark was folly.

But folly often is a friend to young boys. One evening just after dark I entered the bedroom intent upon retrieving an item buried somewhere in a pile on the dresser. Instead of groping for the light string, which was often nearly impossible to find, I chose to brave the hazards of the floor. Almost from the time I entered the room I banged my shins and twisted my ankle on the unseen obstacles scattered across the room. With each new pain and inconvenience, a torrent of profanity escaped from my lips. Before long it seemed every utterance was a profanity. I eventually found the much sought after prize and began a retreat to the door. The return journey proved just as painful and frustrating and the stream of profanity continued.

Just as I reached the door and was about to exit the room, a quiet voice called out from the darkness. "Honey, are you all right?" It was the voice of my mother. She had been lying in the middle of our bed seeking a little solitude in the darkness and had been listening to everything that transpired. Her voice was not angry or threatening. Rather, it betrayed a genuine concern. As I realized my error, I sheepishly replied, "Yes, I'm all right." Of course my head was bowed and shame began to fill my young body from the tip of my toes to the crest of my head. My mother was the last one I would have wanted to surprise in such a way.

That experience helped me to realize that at that moment, I was not living a life that promised any type of fulfillment or satisfaction. I was living a life cluttered with junk. That junk had been carelessly thrown about and I was fumbling around in the darkness, tripping over it. Profanity had become my companion and I had no idea where the light string was hanging. I needed help if my life was to have any purpose or meaning. That help came a few years later when I was introduced to Jesus Christ and embraced him as my Lord and King. Even with Christ in my life though I would not reap the full benefits of his love and sacrifice for me until I grew in my understanding of the bounty that was to be found beneath his cross. The "mother lode" of God's blessing was fastened to a tree waiting for me to discover it.

I was born in a state of sinfulness and was alienated from the very God who was responsible for my existence. The pages that follow are an honest attempt to share the journey of how I have come to understand and know this God who gave his life for me and who would, in time, become the source of my earthly life. He would become my King.

Growing into a Relationship

In committing these thoughts to paper, I realize that some will read and find faults. This is fine. It is not necessary for me that anyone else believe like I believe. I care only that you know what you believe for yourself. Since being introduced to Jesus as a teenager, my single quest has been to grow to know more deeply, the man they call the Son of God. It is in the journey that I have found personal worth and value even in the face of a subjugated status living as an African American in the United States of America. Jesus loves me and gave his life for me so that we could be together. In return, I am growing in my desire and ability to love him back. He is the treasure that God offered to me as proof of his great love. I am the reason he bent the heavens down and came to earth. The same treasure is offered to everyone. My prayer is that you will grow to know the man Jesus for yourself and in that knowledge you will understand how Jesus Christ is God's personal love gift to you.

The Bible has been called the greatest story ever told. Within its pages God has recorded the amazing story of how he made us, lost us and then set in motion a plan to regain us again. It is hard to understand that he would love us so much that he would be willing to sacrifice his own son. It's even more unthinkable that so many reject his offer of Love. For most, the Bible is a big mystery. The mystery becomes a bit more manageable when one stops to consider that the Bibles' intent is to reveal Jesus Christ to us. As we read, we should be reading in such a way that we are seeking Jesus in the various passages and verses of the Old and New Testament. He is not always easy to find but I believe that he is there. This book is designed to help you in your quest to find Jesus in the pages of the Bible and finding him, to grow more deeply in your understanding of him. Here is an example of what I mean.

Studying the Scriptures – (Jesus Christ)

Why wasn't Moses permitted to lead the people of Israel into the Promised Land?

When I ask this question of students and churchgoers I usually get a response similar to "he disobeyed God." They are correct. However, the response is insufficient so I press them for more information. With the prodding they usually tell me that Moses grew angry and in his anger struck the rock when the people of Israel began complaining of their thirst while traversing through the desert. This is also correct. Still, the response just doesn't go deeply enough. At this point the people are usually stumped. What else could I possibly be looking for? The question is unspoken but obvious from the expression on their face. I try to help them by asking, who or what the rock represents? Eventually I just have to tell them. The rock is a "type" of Christ. A "type" is a representational foreshadowing. It is a future picture. In that the rock is a foreshadowing of Christ then one has to look to Christ and his life in order to understand the significance of why Moses would be denied the desire of his heart, by God, because he struck the rock.

In the first instance when the children of Israel complained about their thirst as they roamed through the desert, God instructed Moses to "strike the rock" and water came forth to refresh and nourish the people. On the second occasion when the children of Israel grew thirsty and complained to Moses, he once again went to God with their complaint and was instructed to "speak to the rock". However, Moses was angry and in his anger struck the rock a second time. God honored Moses' prayer and the people's need by letting water flow from the rock a second time however, Moses was punished by being denied the desire of his heart. The reason Moses was punished was because Christ (the rock) came to earth the first time to be smitten by God for man's transgressions. However, when Christ comes the second time he will be coming in power and will never be struck again. God was being intentional when he instructed Moses to "speak" to the rock the second time. Today, Christ is in Heaven seated on a throne next to God the Father. We are instructed to approach the risen Christ in prayer. Whenever we grow thirsty, we are to "speak" to the rock.

In studying the scriptures I have come to understand that it was God's intent that a written word be provided so that we would always have a means to investigate his desire and plan for us. The key to understanding his written word is to seek the savior, Jesus Christ, in every verse. If, when you are studying God's word, you haven't found his son, Jesus, then you haven't studied deeply enough.

Finally, this manuscript is the product of a lifetime of seeking to understand God's great plan for mankind and the vital role that his only son, Jesus Christ, would play in it. I am eternally indebted to all those Saints that have gone before me and been used by the Holy Spirit to bring me to this place of understanding. Any errors or deficiencies in understanding belong only to me with the explanation that God is not finished working with me yet. I love this journey and am grateful to discover others walking along "the way" with me. May our destinations' end find us sitting together at the feet of our Savior and King who one day laid aside his royal robes, and deposited God's blessing beneath Calvary's Cross. A "lode" can be thought of as a rich source of something. That something needs to be mined in order to find the true treasure and as is often true with mining, the deeper you dig the greater the potential bounty. God loves you and has placed the "mother lode" at the feet of his uplifted son. You only need to seek it out.

Part One:
The Beginning of the Journey

Mother's Wisdom

"You need to take off your rose-colored glasses." Mothers' words were spoken from her heart and that troubled me as I watched the slight tear form in the corner of her eyes. I had just returned cross-country from Arizona where I was forced to say goodbye to Amy Bradford. I had gone to Arizona to make Amy, a Bible College love, my wife but her parents violently objected to a union between us because of the color of my skin and in the face of their rejection, Amy and I felt it best that I drive home alone. My face was still slightly bruised and the corner of my lip swollen from the beating I received at the hands of her father. Though I tried to hide it, I knew that my mother saw my pain as I shared with her my most recent experience with Christians. She knew that I had been deeply affected by the experience and now she sought to protect me from further hurt and injury.

Her reference to rose-colored glasses brought a gentle knowing nod. Though I have never been to France, I have heard that in the evenings the lampposts along the thoroughfares of downtown Paris cast a rose-colored haze in the twilight.[i] This causes a surreal effect that is at once beautiful and at the same time otherworldly. Mother was telling me that it was time for me to see my place in the Christian world as it really was.

Encountering White Christians

As I stole away from mother's pitying gaze, my mind flashed back several years to the day the Christians from Youth for Christ first came to our home, asking permission for me to attend their summer camp. Each year they sponsored this camp for delinquent and pre-delinquent boys. I had never had a run-in with the law, but everyone knew that any young black male in my community was never far from that sort of encounter.

The Youth for Christ people assured my mother that other young black boys from the neighborhood would be attending the weeklong camp and I would be well treated. They gained her blessing when they finally shared that there would be no cost to the family for me to attend. Even though my father held a steady job at a local foundry and worked hard, family finances had always been short. I was 15 then and the week at camp opened a whole new world to me -- a Christian world that was unlike anything I'd ever known.

I had come to the attention of Youth for Christ through the three guys with whom I ran. We named ourselves The Horsemen a few years earlier when we acquired matching jackets and pearl handled knives. Now the others had been caught breaking into school lockers to steal the rings, watches and money opposing teams left in their clothes during sporting events. I found out what my friends were doing only when I walked into the high school one morning and was confronted by my wrestling coach. He asked if I had been with them. I didn't know what he was talking about because the guys never shared with me what they were doing. I'd grown up in the black community with a reputation for being an innocent. Even though we often did things that we had no business doing, the others always shielded and protected me from anything illegal. The coach finally let me go on to my homeroom when he was convinced that I hadn't been involved in the thefts.

The arrest of the other Horsemen was the talk of the black community. We were just beginning to make a name for ourselves in sports and the community had great expectations for our futures as athletes. Perhaps that is the reason why, when the others went before the juvenile court judge, he permitted the Youth for Christ people to be in the courtroom and intervene on their behalf. They were headed for either the Christian camp or probation. With the blessing of the judge, the Horsemen agreed to attend the Youth for Christ Lifeline camp and asked whether they could invite a friend. The Youth for Christ people were more than happy to have the guys invite someone else themselves. I was the "friend" that the other Horsemen had in mind.

Youth for Christ Lifeline Camp

The Youth for Christ Lifeline camp was located on Lake Pymatuning about two hours away. We arrived there full of excitement and apprehension. The Horsemen thought that for the week we were at camp we would run the place. In truth we were out of our element and had no idea what was in store for us. The Youth for Christ people had promised that we would have all the food we could eat, all the sports we could play and no preaching. If we had doubts about their promises they vanished when we entered the dining hall to find a veritable banquet.

Stone Age Football

After dinner the 24 campers were divided into two equal cabins and introduced to the camp staff. Our athletic director was a sophomore from Wheaton College named Gil Nichols. Gil was a young, clean-shaven white student who sported a military type crew cut. His plans to enter a military academy after high school ended when he permanently injured a shoulder while playing soccer. Still, he carried himself with the bearing and physique of a military man. After meeting him, the Horsemen knew that our intentions of running the camp might not develop as we had planned.

Gil led the camp to a large open area. Placing two racing cones at each end, he called us to the center of the makeshift football field and explained the rules of the game. "This game is called Stone Age Football. The rules are simple. Cabin A, you defend that goal." He pointed to the north end of the field. "Cabin B, you defend that goal." He pointed to the other end of the field and then added. "There are no other rules."

Gil tossed a football into the air as he made a mad dash for the safety of the sidelines. I don't remember if the ball ever hit the ground. The game was a free-for-all. Anything was permissible so long as the football was carried between the orange cones for a touchdown. I had never seen so many bodies flying through the air and bouncing off the ground in one place before. Anyone who touched the football became the object of the entire camp's attention. It didn't take long to figure out that the strongest, fastest and most versatile would be the ones their teammates would rely on to score the points. For our cabin the Horsemen became those people. We excelled at the game of Stone Age Football and for the first time in my life I knew I was among the absolute best at something. There were other games at the camp--greased watermelon races in the pond, basketball, track & field events, etc.--but it was Stone Age Football that separated the camp into athletes and everyone else.

The third day of camp I learned that there was more to the activities than just fun and games. I had just made my fourth unimpeded pass through the orange cones. Most of the campers simply stepped out of the way when I ran the football. Gil motioned for me to come join him at the sidelines, where he was standing with J. Wendall "Bud" Harmes, the camp director for the week. He then directed my attention to a frustrated, angry little white boy sitting on the ground, pulling grass out by the handful. He told me that this young boy, probably the smallest in the camp, had not been having a very positive experience and then asked if I had any ideas that might help. Almost without thinking I responded, "I know. I'll let him tackle me." Gil and Bud smiled and nodded approvingly. Gil then made his way over to the young boy while I went back out on the field.

The next time I got the football in my hands, I saw a little white blur moving towards me with a reckless type of abandon. When I felt his body impact mine, I used every trick my year of junior varsity wrestling had taught me to flip, roll and bounce off the ground without hurting the little boy attached to my legs. From the ground I could see the pleasure on the boy's face and the satisfaction in the eyes of the camp directors.

Then an amazing thing happened. As soon as the game was started again, one of the other Horsemen ended up with the football and the young boy went after him. With the whole camp watching, he caught my friend, wrapped himself around his legs and brought him to the ground. The camp all but cheered and after that the little boy was treated like a genuine hero. I had never seen such a transformation in a person before and I'd never felt such joy at sacrificing a small part of myself for the benefit of another human being. Perhaps there was more to the camp and the game of Stone Age Football than I had considered.

Why Are They Different?

After the experience on the football field, I began to look at the camp differently. I started to notice things that I had missed. Each morning and night I would see our cabin counselor reading something. When any of us approached, he would quickly slide the book under his pillow and not share what he was reading. During the various athletic activities the counselors were the ones congratulating us on good tackles or well-placed baskets. There was something different about them. They were as rough and tough as we were, but instead of getting angry when we tackled them hard, they would get up and smile while patting us on the back. They prayed before they ate in the dining hall and disappeared after lunch, while we remained in our cabins for an hour of rest. It seemed that they were happy.

When my curiosity finally got the best of me, I made my way to the camp director and shared my observations. I then asked how it was possible for those individuals to be so different from us. Bud only smiled and said we would have a campfire the next night where he would let the guys in question tell us what made them so different. When I shared this information with the other Horsemen, I was surprised to learn that each had noticed the same sort of things, approached the camp director with the same question and received the same response. By the time the campfire was lit the next night all the campers we had spoken with were anxious to hear from our cabin counselors.

Angelic Visitation

The campfire was probably the biggest I'd ever seen. It lit up the evening sky and generated heat sufficient to send all the campers scampering to the safety of felled trees that had been strategically placed around the area. The evening started with hot dogs and marshmallows, accompanied by familiar songs we had been learning all week. Then various cabin counselors stood and told the story of how Jesus had entered their lives and made all the difference for them. I was fascinated. The other campers, including the Horsemen, were indifferent and even bored. Sensing this, the camp directors dismissed the other campers back to their cabins, but I was permitted to stay and talk.

That evening, for the first time in my life, I heard the story of how God made us, lost us, and then personally redeemed us. Gil sat at my side and introduced me to the Savior. It was as though an angel was visiting with me, an angel who was eager for me to understand and embrace what he was saying. We talked for two hours that night. Before the conversation had ended, I knew that God had put on flesh and come to earth. While here, he lived his life loving people and demonstrating how we were all supposed to be with one another. His reward was to be falsely accused by the church of his day, beaten till he was near death, humiliated, rejected and finally killed. Even as he hung on the cross, the instrument of his execution, he still loved people so much that he asked that they be forgiven for their action against him.

I could scarcely believe what I was hearing. I knew there was a pervasive emptiness inside me. I had no one in my life that loved me enough to die for me. I wanted Jesus. My angel, however, wouldn't let me accept Christ that night. Instead he did something that had never been done at Lifeline Camp before. I was asked to come back the following week as his assistant athletic director. I was ecstatic.

Before we parted company that night, Gil told me that he wanted me to promise to come to the Youth for Christ rally on Saturday night instead of going to the community dance. He shared that when I informed the other Horsemen that I would be going to the rally instead of the dance, they would laugh at me. I don't think I believed Gil but I politely smiled and nodded. Gil walked me back to my cabin and wished me a good night. I was tired and sleep came quickly.

The next morning found all of us busily cleaning the campground and preparing to head home. I don't know what I thought about the conversation with Gil. I didn't feel any different and once in the car heading for home, I occupied myself with other areas of conversation with my parents and siblings.

The Conversion

I could hardly wait for Monday to come so that I could return to the camp. I didn't know what to expect because I'd never been an athletic director before. I still had made no decision to receive Christ as personal Savior. Even so I was happy when the car arrived at the campground. I was greeted by the staff and shown where I would be staying. I was to join them for a staff meeting at the picnic table near the dining hall after I was unpacked.

I joined everyone at the table and sat next to "Mac." He was a kindly white-haired old man who made me feel like I was his friend. Everyone shared the events of their weekend. Then they bowed their heads and began to pray aloud around the table. My head began to spin as I realized that it was going to eventually get around to me. I had never prayed out loud before. I had never prayed much beyond "Now I lay me down to sleep."

In no time at all "Mac" was praying beside me. A funny thing happened when he stopped. My mouth opened, the whole world seemed to grow quiet and I heard myself say out loud, "God, I think I've finally found the road." I don't remember what else I said that afternoon. But "Mac" slid over next to me and put his arm around my shoulders. I looked up and saw that he was crying. A soft breeze was blowing and the world looked totally different to me. Before I was done praying, I had accepted Christ into my life but beyond that I had no idea that I had just taken the first step in a life-changing, lifelong journey.

Part Two: "Nothing Personal . . ."

My mother was right. I probably had an unrealistic view of what it meant to be a Christian. Though no one ever talked about it openly with me, there was a sense that we were to worship the Lord Jesus Christ as a non-racial universality. His death mended the breach between the races and through his Spirit we are all united as one family. During those first three years of my Christian walk no one could have convinced me that any other reality was true. Even though I was African American, I had been spot lighted, toasted, and honored by the Christian community that led me into a saving knowledge of Jesus Christ. Because I was coming into my own on the football field and wrestling mat, I could even boast of a small fan club of little white Christian kids across Northwestern Pennsylvania who were reading about me in the newspaper.

After high school graduation my innocent and naïve notions of what it meant to be a Christian changed abruptly when my white spiritual family enrolled me in a Bible School in Arizona. They kept telling me that the school was a break-off of Bob Jones University, of course I had no idea why that would be significant, and that the school was only three years old. I would be their first African American living full time on the campus. My Christian family couldn't have known the type of hell that was awaiting me at that school.

Integrating a Bible School

Upon my arrival and after proper introductions, the school's administration showed me to my new home. It was a converted one-bedroom bungalow with two sets of bunk beds. I soon learned that it was to house four male students and I was the second to arrive. Already situated in the bungalow was a student from Washington State. He introduced himself as Tim and extended a warm hand in greeting to me. Tim and I hit it off immediately and as we shared stories, I found out that he was born in Africa and had a twin brother at home in Seattle. Tim's parents were serving as missionaries in Africa when he was born and had only recently returned to the United States. This African-born white skinned boy who embraced me as a friend fascinated me.

Tim helped me pick out a bunk and unpack the few belongings I brought with me. Soon the front door opened and we were introduced to our third roommate. Abdullah was a Christian from an Arab country. After being introduced to Tim and me, he turned to his sponsor and exclaimed, "See, we now have in this dorm one Arab, one American and one black." I'm not certain that Abdullah knew what he was saying, but the remark stung me and embarrassed Tim. Neither of us tried to correct our Arab roommate and before our first week together had ended, we realized that it was a mistake.

Abdullah's general attitude around me was one of condescension. It was apparent to all that he clearly believed himself to be superior to me. At that time I didn't have any foundation to refute him. I had no experience with anyone other than Americans. I could not understand how it was possible for this young man to come from another country and automatically relegate me to a lesser status.

The fifty students at the institution generally warmed to my presence among them. For many I was the first African American they had ever had an opportunity to get to know in any personal way. Most of the faculty and administration, however, did not share this level of comfort with me.

After only three weeks on campus I met with the president of the school and shared with him my intention to leave and attend a different school. The president of the Bible school pleaded with me not to go and convinced me that I was paving the way for others of my race to attend the institution. I listened to his words and stayed, a decision that began the most intense period of racism and bigotry directed at me that I have ever experienced.

A Different "Christian" Experience

My decision to stay made me the prime object of the institutions negative attention. Parents received phone calls from concerned instructors and administrators if it appeared that I was getting too friendly with any of the female students. Even though I had been one of the best wrestlers in the state of Pennsylvania, I couldn't score better than a C+ in a physical education class. Hateful White supremacy literature was thrown about my car and I found myself often frustrated, humiliated, and angry.

Though it was the late sixties and America was undergoing one of its greatest social transformations, the Bible school had enacted policies that sought to keep the realities of American life outside the campus boundaries. No televisions were allowed on campus, radios could be tuned only to White Christian stations, and rules for leaving and returning to the campus were very restrictive. As students living on campus, we were pretty much cut off from the happenings in the world beyond. Still it was the late 60's and change was everywhere. Even so, I knew that I was alone in a hostile environment.

Just a "Nigger"

"Someone knock that nigger on his ass." The words were supposed to disarm me, I suppose, but they didn't. They had come from the mouth of a 6'5" 250 pound white boy who didn't like the fact that I could play flag football so effectively.

By this time I was a second year student at the small Conservative Baptist Bible School in Arizona. A year earlier, with the help of Bud Harmes and my Youth for Christ friends, I had integrated the school and was still the only black student living in the dorms on campus. On this particular day our school was playing against a prominent church within the denomination. The church, like the denomination, was almost entirely white. The big frustrated boy on the other team was only giving expression to what most on the field were feeling. I played football well, but I was the wrong color.

I had not been able to escape the consequences of my color since becoming a Christian. It was painfully clear to me that I would never be more than a "nigger" to many whom I was now supposed to accept as my brothers and sisters in Christ. Sadly, no one spoke on my behalf that afternoon in the hot Arizona sun, even though the president of the school stood on the sidelines listening and watching to see how I would respond. Sadly, I knew why my color was such a problem for them. In their minds, my black skin showed me to be the recipient of God's curse and therefore I was not worthy of friendship, respect or love. It was an ugly time that left me desperate for any positive relationship. It was then that I met the Bradfords' and their daughter Amy.

A Safe Haven

Amy Bradford was a freshman at the Bible school during my second year. She was also innocent, trusting, very shy and easily angered by the treatment she knew I was experiencing. Hearing about my experiences through their daughter, the Bradfords invited me to their home for dinner and fellowship. There I once more experienced the love and kindness I had known with those who had introduced me to "the Way" a few years earlier. The Bradfords expressed genuine distress over my treatment at the Bible school. They wanted me to know that their home would always be a safe place for me and that all white Christians were not like the ones I was seeing at the school. After each visit in the Bradford home, I left confidant that their love for me was genuine and their home, a legitimate retreat from the harshness of life on campus.

An Unexpected Confrontation

Around campus Amy and I became all but inseparable. Most free time found us playing guitars together in the student lounge, sitting together for meals and talking or praying together in the campus chapel. We made no secret of our trust for each other and felt confident that, because of the support of Amy's parents, the institution was powerless to do anything about the interracial friendship. Unfortunately, we had no idea how determined an objection the institution was prepared to make.

One Saturday afternoon, five weeks into the semester, the Bradfords made an unexpected visit to the school. They found Amy and me playing guitars in the student lounge. Everyone smiled and greeted one another warmly. After a few minutes, Mrs. Bradford took Amy to help unload articles they had brought for her. With the women now gone, Mr. Bradford began a candid conversation with me.

"We've been receiving phone calls saying that you and Amy are dating." His tone was forceful and serious as he looked directly at me, seeking to catch some reaction to his statement. Almost without hesitation I responded that we were friends and did spend a lot of time together but were not romantically involved in any way. In fact, I assured Mr. Bradford, we had never even held hands.

This response pleased him and the tone of the conversation softened. "Mrs. Bradford and I love you and appreciate your friendship with Amy. We don't mind the two of you spending time together so long as there is nothing "social." I knew that I was being told that the Bradfords' did not view me as a suitable mate for their daughter because of the color of my skin. This hurt deeply. I had begun to trust that Amy's parents were different from others I had thus far encountered. They had shown me the most kindness of any since my arrival at the school. The conversation with Mr. Bradford ended abruptly as Amy and her mother reentered the lounge. After 30 minutes of small talk, we escorted them to their car and waved goodbye as they pulled from the parking lot and made their way back home.

After the Bradford's departure, Amy and I talked about the unexpected visit. Amy's face flushed with anger as I told her about my conversation with her father. Then without explanation she turned and darted towards her dorm. We would not see each other again until late that evening. Once together again Amy shared that she had spoken to her parents and learned that they had been receiving almost constant reports from the school since we became friends. Her parents explained that the communications were coming from students, faculty and administration with such urgency that they felt the need to come unannounced to the campus and "see for themselves." We parted that evening deeply saddened by the day's events knowing that we would have to temper our relationship around the small campus.

The next month was torture. I felt like I had lost my closest friend, and the invitations to what had become my safe place ceased. At the same time, the racism directed at me from campus intensified. Now I was truly alone in a hostile place and lacked any resources to leave or any experience base to cope with my situation. Other friends tried to fill the void I felt with the loss of Amy's companionship, but to little avail. I had been made to believe that God had cursed me to be inferior to everyone around me and now I was alone.

An Unexpected Friend

I was out of my element with no place to turn for comfort until I picked up a book by Claude McKay called *Man Child in the Promised Land.* McKay's book opened up a new world to me, and I soon found myself reading everything I could get my hands on about the black experience. Within six months, I was called to the President's office and questioned about the type of materials I was reading. They were concerned that I was becoming a black militant. I wasn't, but there was no way I could have convinced them of that. That meeting helped me to understand that my every action and activity was being monitored and reported to the school's administration. Still, it did not deter me from my readings in the black experience. Beneath the covers of those books the hostile Christian world around me ceased to exist. I found joy in the power of the strong black figures. The heroes who emerged from the pages of those books accepted an inferior status to no man. I liked that, but it was an idea foreign to any reality I had experienced. None of the heroes professed a faith in Jesus Christ as Lord and Savior. How could I possibly be like them and at the same time still profess to belong to Christ?

Crossing a Forbidden Barrier

The self-imposed separation from Amy Bradford ended when she sought me out one evening just before the school's fall break. We hadn't spoken to each other

privately for more than a month, and she wanted me to know that she missed the bond that had formed between us. Throwing all caution to the wind, we made our way to the campus Prayer Chapel and were relieved to discover that no one else was present. Once safely inside, we sat next to each other in silence until Amy slid her hand into mine and gently laid her head on my shoulder. My immediate response was panic, but then I felt myself surrender to feelings buried deep inside and slid my arm around her shoulders. There was no longer any pretense about the affection we felt. We had been friends who cared deeply for one another. That evening marked a turning point in the relationship that we both knew was forbidden, but greatly desired.

Amy and I resumed a very open relationship around campus that once more resulted in strong cries of opposition from many within the institution. This time, however, we simply ignored the voices offering unwanted caution and overt threats. We didn't make an open show of our friendship; neither did we try and hide it. Amy continued to date white classmates, an action that pleased her parents, while I settled into an uneasy peace with my situation. I loved Amy and her parents and, because of their kindness to me, I did not want to do anything that would cause them injury or harm. I would be content with just their friendship if that was all that their context would permit. By Easter, however, it was apparent that the institution's opposition was too strong and had successfully done its work. The Bradfords made it known that they would no longer tolerate any relationship between Amy and me and, as if to reinforce this change, the Bradfords' attitude towards me changed to one of open hostility.

With our relationship under constant scrutiny by the institution and because we were no longer in possession of her parents' blessing, Amy and I once again agreed that for her sake we should not spend time together. I allowed myself to slide into an angry depression that found me hating the color of my skin and the whites that so oppressed me because of it.

In my anger I began to wish I could confront those who introduced me to "Christianity." Was this what they intended when they came to my home to take me to their camp? Didn't they teach me that Christ died to make everyone equal and to break down any walls or barriers between people? Wasn't the Bible supposed to be good news for everyone? How could being cursed by God ever be considered "good news"? Still, because of Amy and a few other students who continued to defy classmates and administration in order to befriend me, I was forced to temper this bitterness and seek solitude in a self-world of personal remorse. Where was the Christ who found me and placed me on the road to heaven?

A Providential Encounter

One afternoon towards the end of the school year, Tom Skinner, the noted black evangelist, appeared on campus. Earlier in the year he had been conducting crusades in the city and was invited to speak in a chapel service at the school. He was uninvited when students complained to the administration that he fellowshipped with liberals. On this day Skinner came to the campus unannounced because he was curious to see what type of school it was. From a window in my bungalow I saw him walking across the grounds and ran out to introduce myself to him. Upon seeing me, he motioned for me to walk with him to a private area. Once we were alone, he suggested to me that I needed to transfer to a different institution. I listened to Tom Skinner that afternoon and during the summer, while working at a Youth for Christ Lifeline Camp in Indiana, tried to transfer out of the Bible school. I chose a school in Indiana a few hours from the camp and wrote the Bible school requesting that my transcripts be forwarded.

One month later I received a letter from the new institution informing me that my transcripts had been sent to them from Arizona with a bright red stamp stating that I had been suspended for disciplinary reasons. The letter then went on to explain that I would not be able to transfer to any Christian college in the nation until the suspension was lifted. I knew nothing about a suspension, so I called the Bible school, only to be informed that, if I wanted any information, I needed to make a special trip back to the school for a hearing.

Gil Nichols, who had been trying to help me transfer, called the school and asked about the suspension. He was told that I was suspended for "indiscretions with white girls." Upon further inquiry the leadership at the Bible school informed him that I had violated the school's "six inch rule" and had been seen holding hands with a girl on campus. The charge was true. Against my better judgment, I fell in love with Amy and had held her hand in a public place at the school.

When the phone call ended, I heard Gil curse beneath his breath. There were tears in his eyes and he excused himself from the room without speaking to me. After an hour he returned and apologized. The phone call had made him so angry with the school that he couldn't speak to anyone. At that moment I knew that Christ was not absent from my circumstances and had permitted Gil Nichols, the man who had introduced me to the Lord, to touch a portion of my pain. I wasn't alone after all.

One month after this conversation I received another letter from the school to which I was trying to transfer. The letter was an apology and an acceptance. I learned later that Gil had contacted national Christian leaders and informed them of my plight. The new school received letters and phone calls from leaders like Tom Skinner, Bill Pannell, and Jay Kesler, all pleading my cause.

That fall I began my college career all over again at a Christian college in the Mid-west, but the experience in Arizona had done its work. I was broken inside and white Christians had become the cause of my brokenness. A large number of the white Christians with whom I had had contact to that point truly believed themselves to be my superior and no social status, class standing or spiritual condition could alter my inferiority in their minds. It was sealed in the pigmentation of my skin.

A Fresh Start

Anderson University was a breath of fresh air for me. It did have rules and a code of conduct, but they were nothing like the conservative Bible School I had just left. The college was home to nearly two-dozen African-American students and boasted two black professors. In the welcoming atmosphere of that institution, I began to experience a sense of healing. I was black, but few there seemed to mind.

My joy at being a student at the school increased the moment I looked at the course offerings and saw Black History as one of the available classes. I enrolled in the course without hesitation and soon found myself seated in a moderate sized auditorium with about forty other students awaiting the arrival of the professor.

My wait was soon rewarded by the presence of a well-groomed African-American male who stood at the podium in front of the class and introduced himself as our instructor. Then, without waiting for a reaction, he turned and began writing on the chalkboard behind him a phrase that helped me to understand why my personal journey through America was so difficult: "Not one institution in America was conceived, structured or, today, functions with any other people in mind than the white man."

Immediately, the hands of anxious white students shot up around the room and I felt a strange sense of enlightenment and satisfaction. With a single sentence the professor had managed to capture and give expression to my frustration. It was a frustration I did not know how to express without anger. But the professor didn't appear angry and responded to the students' inquiries with a measured, self-confident tone.

The content of that class and the professor's gentleness with the students who obviously struggled with some of the things he said convicted me about my lack of knowledge about my own journey through America as an African American and my feelings towards some of the whites I had encountered. My ancestors were slaves, brought to America against their will and in chains. It was a reality that I could do nothing about except seek God's intent for my presence in a land where I was now free, but did not feel wanted.

The Letter

Though months had passed and I was experiencing a sense of personal renewal, I couldn't get Amy out of my mind. She, more than any other, seemed hurt by my decision to leave Arizona. Had she returned to the Bible school? Was she still suffering because of her friendship with me? Were her parents still mad at me for the trouble I brought into their lives? I knew these questions would remain unanswered; I could not risk further injury to Amy's life by writing to her. Then her letter came. I recognized Amy's handwriting as soon as I saw the envelope and knew that I needed a private place before I could open and read it. Alone in the privacy of my dorm room, excitement and joy flooded my body as I read of the pain my absence brought and of the deep love Amy held for me. I knew that I deeply loved her as well and to deny, run, or hide from that truth was futile. Without further thought of consequences, I made my way to a telephone and called her.

Our conversation brought tears to our eyes. It was true, we loved each other and the separation had only intensified our longing to be reunited. It isn't clear who proposed to whom but before the phone call was ended, Amy and I had pledged to be wed. Together we agreed to spend the remainder of the year apart and then reunite and wed during the summer months when I could travel back to Arizona to pick her up. Subsequent phone calls only served as confirmation that we were doing the right thing.

The Reunion

The year passed slowly for the two of us but finally the school term ended and I soon found myself driving back to Arizona to be with Amy. Then, three long days later I checked into a motel near her home and phoned her. Amy was excited that I was so near and rushed to the motel to be with me. The year of separation gave way to hugs, smiles and kisses as soon as Amy walked through the motel door. I could not remember experiencing such joy. With our reunion complete, we immediately began to make plans for a future as husband and wife.

The Pronouncement

Amy knew that her parents would not approve of our union and offered to secretly pack her few belongings overnight and then leave with me the next morning. We would simply inform her parents after the wedding was complete. However, as the afternoon gave way to evening and our conversation became more reflective, we remembered how loving and supportive her parents had been towards me as a young black stranger in their home. We determined that we needed to honor those early efforts and sit to talk with the Bradfords before we could leave to be married. That evening, as we talked and planned further, something moved me to say aloud, "no matter what happen, I won't hit him back." Neither of us knew why I said it and we both looked at each other perplexed. Amy was the first to speak, "you were a champion athlete. My father would never dream of doing anything to you." Of course she was right, it was a silly pronouncement that we soon shrugged off.

The Plan

We decided we would tell her parents of our plan during lunch the next day. Together we agreed to meet at Amy's home the next morning after siblings had gone to school and parents to work. We would then pack her belongings into my car, return to the motel and wait for her parents to return home for lunch. Amy would meet them alone and break the news to them, and then I was to arrive fifteen minutes later to pick her up so that if the parents wanted to talk, we could have a conversation and if not, we could just leave. After we finalized the plan, Amy left for the night, excited, anxious and a bit scared.

Parent's Respond

The next morning Amy returned to the motel and we waited together until time for us to retrieve her belongings. It had been over a year and a half since my last visit to the Bradford home and, once inside, it felt strange being there alone with Amy. The atmosphere in the home was thick with tension as we busied ourselves gathering her things -- neither of us made any effort to lessen it. Neither of us knew how. Once her things were packed safely into my car, we returned to the motel to wait for the time for Amy to break the news to her parents.

The hours passed slowly but when, at last the time for her departure arrived our anxious anticipation gave way to a sense of relief. I walked Amy to her car, smiled and waved as I watched her pull out of the parking lot and head towards her home. Soon her parents would know of our plans and we would be off to start our life together. Fifteen minutes after Amy left, I started my own car and began the short drive to the Bradford House. As I pulled in front of the home I could see two cars in the driveway and Mr. Bradfords' truck sitting diagonal across the front lawn. He obviously had come home in a great hurry.

The Beating

With an unexpected sense of dread I got out of my car and started up the walk to the enclosed porch of the house. The door to the porch had been left wide open so I walked through to the front door of the house and stopped at its threshold. Like the door on the porch it too had been left ajar and from where I was standing I could see past the dining room and into the living room area. Amy was seated on the sofa with her mother standing over her. Each time Amy tried to rise, her mother would push her back into the sofa. I knocked on the door to announce my presence and heard Amy shout out, "you better not hurt him." Then, as I took a step into the house, I caught a glimpse of movement to my left. I jerked my head in the direction of the movement just in time to see Amy's father rushing at me with his fists flailing at the air. I had just enough time to lift his hands and arms to cover my face when Mr. Bradfords' punches began to land. Amy's father was shouting something incoherent to me as he continued to beat me. While Mr. Bradfords' blows were striking various parts of my body, I slowly backed from the front door, through the enclosed porch, down the steps, across the sidewalk and finally into the middle of the street.

All the while I was being pelted by Mr. Bradfords' blows one thought kept repeating itself in my head, "no matter what happens, I won't hit him back." The thought kept me restrained in the face of the punishment my body was receiving and I found myself trying to talk to the angry white man who had once proclaimed his love for me. When Amy's father finally stopped beating and kicking at me, I looked past him and could see that Amy and her mother had both exited the house and were watching from the lawn. Amy's mother was physically restraining her from coming to my aid but I could see that she was all right and this brought a sense of relief. As Amy's father retreated back towards her, she gave a signal to me that meant I was to go back to the motel and wait. She would come to meet me when she was able. I nodded a reluctant agreement and returned to my car. It wasn't until I was safely in the motel room that I relaxed enough to taste the blood in my mouth and feel the bruises where the blows had made contact. As I assessed how little physical damage I sustained during the ordeal, I began to experience a sense of satisfaction in the knowledge that I did not raise a fist and strike Amy's father back. I had remained in control of myself. Then, not knowing what else to do, I laid down across the bed curled into a neo-natal ball and rocked myself asleep.

"I Can't Go With You"

It was dark when I woke up to the bright lights of a car pulling into a parking spot at the entrance to the room. I barely had time to turn a light on when Amy pushed the sliding glass door open and fell into my arms. As I held her she began crying out, "I can't go with you." I responded, "I know. It's all right. Your parents need you more right now more than I do. But I'll never be able to come back and get you." With that we sat on the edge of the bed and cried together. I had never permitted another human being to see me cry like that but I was bruised and broken. As I laid my head on her lap, she stroked my hair to comfort me and gently told me what had happened after I left.

Amy explained that her father collapsed and broke into tears before he could get back into the house. Her mother helped him inside and then made a call to their family minister who came immediately to talk with and comfort them. Much to their surprise, the family minister explained to the Bradford parents that they were wrong to forbid the marriage. Scripture did not support their actions. He then advised that they pull the family together around their "family-alter" and discuss the situation. Amy locked herself in the bathroom while the minister was speaking to her parents and refused to come out until all were assembled for their alter. After everyone was made aware of the events of the afternoon, they went around the room one by one and shared their thoughts. When everyone had had a chance to speak the Bradfords tearfully turned to Amy and told her that she could leave and get married if she wanted but that they wished she would remain at home with them for just one year longer. Amy could see that her parents were hurting and struggling to find a way to do the right thing so she agreed to stay with the provision that she be permitted to return to the motel alone and share her decision with me. When she finished speaking we held each other in silence until it was time to transfer her belongings to her own car and say a final goodbye.

The Long Trip Home – Alone

After Amy's departure I checked out of the motel and began a lonely drive back across country. It was a long silent drive. Leaving Amy behind was the most difficult thing I had ever had to do and soon I found myself questioning whether or not it was the right decision.

The drive ended at the front door of my parent's home. I didn't know where else to go. As I sat in their driveway, I wondered, "how much should I tell them?" They had never said much about the Christian walk I had found. Nor had they prevented me from becoming involved with the Christian group that had adopted me. Mother often told me stories about how her father had served as a janitor in the downtown church of the white Christians before they left to build their country chapel. They knew my grandfather to be a godly man and permitted him to stand in the balcony to observe as they worshipped. Perhaps mother would have words of wisdom now. Before I had a chance to reflect any further, mother opened the front door and anxiously beaconed for me to come in. Before I could get to the porch I could tell from the look on her face that mother already knew something wasn't right with me. The dark glasses I donned were not going to be enough to hide my hurt from her.

Once inside I told mother my sad tale and was advised to take off my rose colored glasses. She was right. If I were going to be a true follower of the Lord Jesus Christ, then I needed to figure out who Jesus Christ was for me as a black male living in the United States of America in the midst of one of its greatest social revolutions. What was it all supposed to mean for me? As I pondered that question, the Holy Spirit gently prodded my heart to recall the occasions when, as an early Christian, I was asked what happened to me after my conversion. I now know that that prodding was the first steps of a journey to help me discover the treasure God had buried for me to find.

I was only home for two days when I got a phone call from Gil. He called to remind me that I was expected in Indianapolis the following weekend to go to work at their Lifeline Camp. I tried to beg out of the obligation but Gil persisted and the next morning I found myself in my car heading for my summer job.

What Happened to You?

On three separate occasions the question of what happened to me when I met Christ was posed and on three separate occasions I failed to give an adequate response because I was too immature in my faith and too uninformed about the meaning of Christ's sacrifice to answer intelligently.

The Camp Director

The first time I was asked for an explanation of what happened to me occurred the third Tuesday in August 1965, the day after my conversion. As I exited the dining hall shortly after breakfast, Ray Curry, Jr., a local Evangelist and camp director for the week, blocked my path to the cabins and demanded to know, *what happened to you?* I had never had a conversation with this director before and because of the force behind his question, thought that I had done something to get me into trouble. As earnestly as I could, I replied, "nothing." Ray just turned and walked away. Nothing more was said to me until the next day when he confronted me once again as I was leaving the dining hall, *what happened to you?* This time when I replied "nothing," Ray stopped me and said, "You became a Christian," and placed a small red pocket new testament in my hands. Even though the little Bible was written in King James English, I found myself drawn to the Book of Romans and was surprised to discover that I understood some of the things that I was reading. Though we continued to encounter each other daily, Ray Curry, Jr. never again asked me that question but would smile each time our paths crossed.

The Horsemen

One week after I returned home from the camp, the other "Horsemen" came to the house and invited me to spend the night with them at an old Cub Scout campground not far from where we lived. I accepted. I was glad to be with the guys once more but something was different about the relationship – a difference not so much stated as felt. The four of us horsed around as usual, ate stolen watermelon, and told stories around a small campfire, late into the night. Then the next morning one of the guys rekindled the fire and produced bacon and eggs for everyone. The food was wonderful but more significant to me was their inquiry. "What happened to you?" There was a genuine curiosity in the voice. I knew immediately that they were asking what happened to me after they went back into the cabin and I remained at the campfire talking to Gil. I told them that I wasn't sure but that something was different inside of me. The other Horsemen smiled, patted me on the shoulder and wished me well. I knew that they were telling me goodbye. That morning, though we would remain friends, my days as a Horseman ended. The third time I was asked for an explanation as to why I was different marked the beginning of an intentional growth process in me to learn to share the Christ who found me.

The "Bird"

"I've been watching you for a while now and you're different from the days when we used to run together. Also, you carry that Bible on top of your books. Can you tell me what it's all about? What happened to you?"

I was totally unprepared for the bird's question. I had just sat down in a 12th grade English class. The questioner was Bob Boyer. We had spent the last two years of our elementary school days running the streets of our community together. It was there that he had earned his nickname: The Bird.

Bob liked to climb to the tops of trees and ride the branches as they bent down to the ground. We were both known as wild in those days, but lost contact when we started junior high school.

I now sat in my seat stunned. I was a high school football and wrestling star and, as a new Christian two years into the faith, had been trained to carry my Bible high and proud. No one had ever asked my why before.

I grew embarrassed at the attention we were receiving and put The Bird off, explaining that we would talk about it another time. In truth, I didn't know what to say to him. Bob and I would never again have an opportunity to talk about it. A few weeks before graduation, on the night of the prom,

Bob tried to climb to the top of one of the highest trees in the woods while at a beer party. The branch broke off as he tried to ride it to the ground. He died instantly when his head hit the hard dirt. I have never forgotten that he one day asked me for a reason for my hope.

I got serious about the Word of God after that. I never again wanted to be embarrassed by someone asking me why I was different. Since that day, I've always felt that two people had to die for Rick Gray. The first died to save my soul, and the second, to make me get serious about my profession of faith. After the bird's death I began to study the scriptures and to learn for myself what the journey I had embraced was to mean for my living and conversation.

The First Stirrings of Growth

Some years after leaving her in Arizona, Amy Bradford would find me in Seminary and begin a written correspondence. She would be in her third marriage and I would be working towards a doctorate having completed two Masters degrees. She shared with her parents that we were in communications and her father sent a message to me through her. The message simply said "Nothing personal, just not in my family." The years and level of accomplishments had not dulled the bigotry and prejudice. Didn't he understand whose family I belonged to? When I didn't strike him back the day of the beating, I fell in love with the Lord in earnest and I grew to realize just how deeply he loved me. Years of training and conditioning on the football field and wrestling mat helped me to understand that I could have ended Mr. Bradfords' assault with a single blow. But I made an intentional decision not to raise my hand against him. Just as the Lord made an intentional decision not to use the power available to him to end the assault against his life that fateful day in Jerusalem. I understood in a very real way, the kind of restraint Jesus exercised that day and because I was able to exercise the same type of restraint, realized that on that day in the streets of Arizona, I began to grow up in Christ and stopped being a child.

Study and personal reflection have brought me to a place where I now understand that this journey through life is not about running a race and crossing the finish line first. Rather, the journey is about learning to love to run. The chapters that follow are the "good news" that I wish I would have known how to communicate when I was asked what happened to me at Calvary and what I would tell the "bird" if I had the opportunity today.

"Jesus Christ, as the Living Word, was there with God in the beginning"

Part Three: In the Beginning, God!!

We begin our story where the Bible begins, "In the beginning . . ." Genesis 1:1[1] tells us that at the start of all things, God created the heavens and the earth. St. John's gospel informs us that Jesus Christ, as the Living Word, was there with God in the beginning (John 1:1,2)[2] and, in fact, was the one who created everything (John 1:3)[3]. It is not difficult to believe that the original creation was very beautiful. Even today we get glimpses of this beauty and draw hope and inspiration from it that our tomorrows will be better than today. As a part of this creation, we have come to understand that Jesus created powers, rulers and authorities. Included in this must be the Angels (Col. 1:16,17)[4]. Because Angels are not given in sex, it is probable that all of the Angels were called into being at the same time (Psalms 148:5)[5]. An innumerable host of Angels were created, not from dust like human beings, but from a substance of which we are not informed.

---

[1] Gen. 1:1 In the beginning God created the heavens and the earth.

[2] John 1:1 In the beginning was the Word, and the Word was with God, and the Word was God.
1:2 He was with God in the beginning.

[3] John 1:3 Through him all things were made; without him nothing was made that has been made.

[4] Col. 1:16 For by him all things were created: things in heaven and on earth, visible and invisible, whether thrones or powers or rulers or authorities; all things were created by him and for him.
1:17 He is before all things, and in him all things hold together.

[5] Psa. 148:5 Let them praise the name of the LORD, for he commanded and they were created.

Angels were created with different levels of authority, rankings and classifications. Scriptures identify for us at least four different classes of angelic beings. These are called Cherubim (Genesis 3:24)[6], Seraphim (Isaiah 6:2,6)[7], Archangels (Jude 9)[8] and Living Creatures (Revelations 4:6)[9]. At the head of all of the Angels was Lucifer.

I came from a larger family. There were nine of us and with my father being the only source of income in the home, so it was not surprising that one of us would be tapped to live with my grandmother after the death of my grandfather.

I was ten years old when I moved in with her and was immediately introduced into the life of St. John's Missionary Baptist Church. The Church was grandmother's life and by the time I began attending, she had grown to the place where she

---

[6] Gen. 3:24 So he drove out the man; and he placed at the east of the garden of Eden Cherubims, and a flaming sword which turned every way, to keep the way of the tree of life.

[7] Is. 6:2 Above it stood the Seraphims: each one had six wings; with twain he covered his face, and with twain he covered his feet, and with twain he did fly.

[8] Jude 9 Yet Michael the archangel, when contending with the devil he disputed about the body of Moses, durst not bring against him a railing accusation, but said, The Lord rebuke thee.

[9] Rev. 4:6 Also before the throne there was what looked like a sea of glass, clear as crystal. In the centre, around the throne, were four living creatures, and they were covered with eyes, in front and behind (niv).

was recognized as the "church mother." In the Black Church this is a place of high honor. Grandmother led the choir processional every Sunday for worship service and sat in the number one choir chair. Of course I didn't realize the significance of all of this at the time. But I did know that everyone spoke kindly to grandmother and anytime there was a visiting minister at the church, he and his family would stay in our home and take their meals with us. I also learned that grandmother was going to make me go to church with her every Sunday whether I liked it or not and that I couldn't go to bed at night without first saying a prayer.

The prayer I was taught was simple. "Now I lay me down to sleep, I pray the Lord my soul to keep. If I should die before I wake, I pray the Lord my soul to take." She taught it to me word for word and I repeated it each night until I knew it and believed it from my heart. Never a night passed that found me in bed before saying that prayer. The other thing grandmother gave to me was a profound belief that Angels were real and that God had given them charge to watch over me in my sleep. I liked the security I felt in knowing that Angels were protecting me. As I grew older in my grandmother's home I contented myself with the knowledge that my grandfather was an Angel in heaven and after my death, the Lord would make me an Angel too.

I'm sure it was the influence of the St. John's Missionary Baptist Sunday School's lessons that I had learned and grandmothers watchful urgings that caused me truly to believe that being an Angel was to be more desired than being a mere human being. Angels were known to be stronger than men. They were more intelligent and could fly. Not only did they possess those wonderful attributes, but they also went about helping people for God. I cannot express how much I longed to be one of God's Angels after my death like my grandfather. For a long time after my conversion, I was disappointed when I learned that humans don't become Angels when they die. In my youth, I would accuse Lucifer of turning bad, becoming Satan, making God angry and spoiling it for everyone.

Today, the youthful anger has been replaced by a profound joy that can only come with growth. Satan was a murderer from the start and the evil that was in his heart did not need to be a part of my life's experience. God had a better plan for me and only by walking in surrender to his will would I be able to embrace it and one day become a part of his royal and holy family. As an adopted son I would be elevated above the Angels of heaven.

Lucifer – the Son of the Morning

"The Devil made me do it." The comedian Flip Wilson made that statement a hallmark of one of his comedic sketches. Anytime Geraldine was naughty, her excuse became the devil. As a child we all learned that the devil was real, scary and very bad.

The Bible tells us that Lucifer (or Satan), our adversary, was once the highest ranking of all the created beings. He was both wise and beautiful to the eye (Ex. 28: 12)[10], who of us in this world of ours doesn't desire those twin attributes. Our world values wisdom and our world values good looks. Those who possess both often rise to places of honor and seldom want for anything. In some measure the same must have been true for heaven. Lucifer had it all. The Creator gave to him a keen mind, physical attractiveness and power. As head of all the created beings, those under his authority would have held Lucifer in deep reverence. It is not unreasonable to assume that it was because of his wisdom, looks and power that pride rose up in him. The Bible describes his pride as a self-pride (Ezekiel 28:17)[11], and that this pride would ultimately be his undoing.

---

[10] Ex. 28: 12 Thus saith the Lord GOD; Thou sealest up the sum, full of wisdom, and perfect in beauty.

[11] Ex. 28:17 Thine heart was lifted up because of thy beauty, thou hast corrupted thy wisdom by reason of thy brightness: I will cast thee to the ground, I will lay thee before kings, that they may behold thee.

Pride has been identified as one of the seven deadly sins that still effect mankind. God in his graciousness gives blessing and gifts to man. Few of us who are on the receiving end of His blessing are able to resist the pride that fills us and threatens to lessen God's good work in us. Lucifer with all of his power was unable to resist and because of it, sinned a sin that would change God's created order.

Lucifer's home or the place, from which he ruled, was Eden, the garden of God (Ezekiel 28:13)[12]. Not only did he live in the garden of God and rule from there, he also held authority over a large number of Angels.

Because of his self-pride and vanity, Lucifer determined to ascend into heaven from the garden of God and set himself up as the sole ruler upon the throne of God. This is clearly seen in his pronouncements of Isaiah 14:13-14. Lucifer states:

- I will ascend into heaven,
- I will exalt my throne above the stars of God;
- I will sit upon the mount of the congregation;
- I will ascend above the heights of the clouds;
- I will be like the most High.[13]

---

[12] Ex. 28:13   Thou hast been in Eden the garden of God;

[13] Is. 14:13 For thou hast said in thine heart, I will ascend into heaven, I will exalt my throne above the stars of God: I will sit also upon the mount of the congregation, in the sides of the north:
14:14 I will ascend above the heights of the clouds; I will be like the most High.

God permitted Lucifer to traffic this mutiny throughout the heaven realm (Ezekiel 28:18)[14] until as many as one third of the Angels were willing to join him in his overthrow attempt (Revelation 12:4)[15].

John Milton, in his classic book, *Paradise Lost*, suggests that there was war in heaven. This war occurred when the Angels who were loyal to Lucifer battled with the Angels loyal to the Eternal Living One. Finally, according to Milton, when God was satisfied that all of the Angels loyal to Lucifer, were fighting at his side, he sent his son (the pre-incarnate Jesus Christ) forth in his power to oust Lucifer and his followers from

the heavenly realm. So great was the power in which this pre-incarnate Jesus Christ came, that *just his appearance* was sufficient to send Lucifer and the evil Angels over the sides of heaven and into the outer darkness.

---

[14] Ex. 28:18 Thou hast defiled thy sanctuaries by the multitude of thine iniquities, by the iniquity of thy traffick;

[15] Rev. 12:4 And his tail drew the third part of the stars of heaven, and did cast them to the earth:

Scripture tells us that the force of the fall of Lucifer and his evil band was so great that destruction was everywhere. Nations were weakened, kingdoms were shaken and everywhere there was chaos (Isaiah 14:16-17)[16].

Satan (the fallen Lucifer) lost his place of dominion and authority. The Garden of Eden lost its tenant. While no one can be certain, it is probable that the fall of Lucifer happened somewhere between Genesis 1:1 and Genesis 1:2. Some support for this view is offered in Isaiah 24:1[17] and in the book of Jeremiah 4:23[18]. With this in mind, the phrase "And the Spirit of God moved upon the face of the waters," should be understood as an act of re-creation.

After his fierce anger that resulted in the judgment and expulsion of Lucifer and his evil legions, had been satisfied, God began to make anew that which had existed before but was now in chaos.

---

[16] Is.14:16 They that see thee shall narrowly look upon thee, and consider thee, saying, Is this the man that made the earth to tremble, that did shake kingdoms;
14:17 That made the world as a wilderness, and destroyed the cities thereof;

[17] Is. 24:1 Behold, the LORD maketh the earth empty, and maketh it waste, and turneth it upside down,

[18] Jer. 4:23 I beheld the earth, and, lo, it was without form, and void; and the heavens, and they had no light.

To the human mind it is incomprehensible that Lucifer, a created being, could possibly think that he could ascend and take God's place. Or, that so many who shared God's presence could be persuaded to follow Lucifer in his rebellion.

There is a temptation to want to hate Lucifer, to blame his failure for the cause of all of our own individual misery. Yet each of us in his own way has winked at Satan's rebellion. He defied the Most High God and opened the door for each of us to defy him as well.

The Crown of God's Creation

After God caused his spirit to move upon the face of the waters, he called forth light. We know that God is light (I John 1:5)[19] darkness has nothing to do with him. So another way of thinking about it might be to say God stepped into the darkness and it gave way to his presence. He called the light day and the darkness night (Genesis 1:5)[20]. God then called forth the firmament or heavens, followed by land, the sea and plant life. Next came the sun, the moon, and the stars. Finally, came animal life, followed by the creation of man, in God's image, on the sixth day (Genesis 1:27)[21].

God is eternal and infinite. This means that he has always existed and always will exist. More than that, death can have no part with God because he is life itself. This is important because we read in Genesis 2:7;

---

[19] I John 1:5 This then is the message which we have heard of him, and declare unto you, that God is light, and in him is no darkness at all.

[20] Gen. 1:5 And God called the light Day, and the darkness he called Night. And the evening and the morning were the first day.

[21] Gen. 1:27 So God created man in his own image, in the image of God created he him; male and female created he them.

And the Lord God formed man of the dust of the ground, and breathed into his nostrils the breath of life; and man became a living soul.

In an act unduplicated throughout the re-creation story, God bent low over man and breathed the breath of life into his nostrils. It is God's breath in each of us that will live forever. When man became a living soul, a part of him became everlasting. Though each of us has a definite beginning, a portion of us will live forever.

The re-creation account continues. Adam (which means "man") was placed eastward in the Garden of Eden, along with the tree of Life and the tree of the knowledge of good and evil (Genesis 2:8,9)[22].

The loving God who made and gave life to man, knew that the simple tasks involved in maintaining the garden of Eden would not be sufficient to keep him from loneliness. Therefore God resolved to make a helpmate for him (Genesis 2:18)[23].

---

[22] Gen. 2:8 And the LORD God planted a garden eastward in Eden; and there he put the man whom he had formed.
2:9 And out of the ground made the LORD God to grow every tree that is pleasant to the sight, and good for food; the tree of life also in the midst of the garden, and the tree of knowledge of good and evil.

[23] Gen. 2:18 And the LORD God said, It is not good that the man should be alone; I will make him an help meet for him.

God caused a deep sleep to fall over Adam and as he slept, the Eternal One pulled a single rib from his side and molded it into a woman. When this task was completed, God presented this bride to Adam. This portion of the re-creation narrative ends with the simple statement that man and woman were both naked but were not ashamed (Genesis 2:25)[24].

It is probable that the first man and the first woman had no reason to be ashamed because God (who is light, and who dwells in a light so bright that he can't be seen) covered Adam and his bride with a light of their own. This light was probably similar to the one that was emitted by the Lord Jesus Christ at his transfiguration (Matthew 17:2)[25]. This light will also shine from us in our glorified resurrection bodies.

Man and woman loved each other and prospered as the new tenants of God's garden.

---

[24] Gen. 2:25 And they were both naked, the man and his wife, and were not ashamed.

[25] Matt. 17:2 And was transfigured before them: and his face did shine as the sun, and his raiment was white as the light.

Enter the Devil

The dethroned Lucifer (now called Satan) probably watched Adam and Eve in the garden and recalled how he had once held dominion and control over the earth. He reasoned (rightly, I might add) that if he could entice the new inhabitants of Eden to disobey the Creator's instructions to them, then perhaps, the authority he once held over the earth would return to him.

To execute his plan Genesis 3:1[26] informs us that Satan took the form of a serpent (meaning shining one) after he re-entered the garden and waited. His wait was soon rewarded, for he was able to initiate his assault against Eve as she walked in the garden.

---

[26] Gen. 3:1 Now the serpent was more subtle than any beast of the field which the LORD God had made. And he said unto the woman, Yea, hath God said, Ye shall not eat of every tree of the garden?

Scripture records that the attack on Eve consisted of Satan putting doubt into her mind concerning the truth of God's spoken word. (Gen 3:4)[27]. Satan succeeded in causing Eve to doubt her faith in God's word and in making her believe the same lie that had been the cause of his downfall. He made Eve believe that she could be like God. Satan probably chose Eve as the instrument of his attack because, unlike Adam who received the instructions regarding the forbidden fruit directly from God, she received the warning second hand from Adam.

With Satan's encouragement, Eve bit into the fruit of the forbidden tree. Immediately the state of innocence in which she had always existed was gone. Immediately the radiant light (God's glory reflecting from her person) that had been her covering vanished.

Eve's action separated her from her Creator. The fallen woman probably was stunned, bewildered and in a state of confusion as she slowly turned toward Adam. We can easily believe that Adam instantly would have realized what she had done because her radiant light was now gone. At that point, Adam was as far removed from Eve as righteousness is from sin.

---

[27] Gen. 3:4 And the serpent said unto the woman, Ye shall not surely die:

As Eve arrived at where Adam stood, the forbidden fruit still in hand, Adam's heart broke. He remembered the Lord's warning and now could plainly see the consequences of not obeying God's word. Adam saw no sorrow or remorse in his wife's eyes. No tears of sadness. Rather, he sensed a strange satisfaction in Eve's face. Eve stood before Adam and explained what she had done. She shared with him how good the strange fruit tasted. Adam gazed at the fruit she held in her hand and then toward heaven as the quiet inner voice within his head gently reminded him of God's warning and admonition. He remembered, with joy, the happiness he had shared with his creator. He remembered how they had walked and laughed and talked the day he brought all of the animals for him to name. He remembered, too, that strange sensation of loneliness, that twinge of incompleteness that would sometimes creep over him as he played with the animals. He remembered the love with which God laid him down upon the ground and caused a deep sleep to engulf him. And he remembered his surprise and satisfaction when his wife was presented to him. How happy those memories were. A tear probably rolled down his cheek as he made up his mind to join his mate in her fallen, sinful state.

Deliberately, he stretched out his hand and took the partially eaten fruit from Eve. In willful disobedience to God's word, Adam quickly placed the fruit in his mouth and ate. Immediately, Adam's light was also gone. His innocence gave way to the knowledge of right and wrong and he began to look at the world and at his wife with a different kind of sight. The writer of Genesis tells us:

And the eyes of them both were opened,
and they knew that they were naked Genesis 3:7.

"Adam, Where are you?"

After partaking of the forbidden fruit, the light that emanated from the bodies of Adam and Eve and which served as their covering, disappeared. Their innocence also disappeared and the Bible tells us that they knew that they were naked. Knowing that God made a habit of walking in the Garden of Eden in the cool of the evening with him, Adam tried to cover his nakedness with fig leaves and then hid himself. Eve did the same. When God arrived and did not find Adam waiting for him, Genesis records that he called out to him "Adam, where are you?" It is usually supposed that God was calling out for Adam to reveal his location but God didn't need that information from Adam. He is God and knows everything. Rather, I think God was asking Adam what happened to their relationship. They had been communing in fellowship when suddenly the fellowship was broken and God knew that Adam had sinned. God wanted Adam to reflect on the fact that their relationship was different.

Sinful Separation

Nothing in creation was spared the consequences of Adams decision to turn his back on God (Roman 8:22)[28]. However, it was humanity that would bear the brunt of Adams and Eve's failure. In the book of Romans we read, "Wherefore, as by one man sin entered the world, and death by sin, so death passed upon all men, for that all have sinned." (Romans 5:12)[29]. This is called the theory of *Federal Head-ship* and means that because of Adam's willful, deliberate decision to join his wife in her fallen state, sin and its consequences has become the natural state for all men. Now, both Adam and Eve have sinned, however, Adam's fall was the greater and sin has passed to all of us today through him, and not through the female.

---

[28] Rom. 8:22 For we know that the whole creation groaneth and travaileth in pain together until now.

[29] Rom. 5:12 Wherefore, as by one man sin entered into the world, and death by sin; and so death passed upon all men, for that all have sinned:

The explanation is simple. Woman was beguiled. Eve had always existed in a state of innocence and was deceived by Satan when she believed his lie. Adam, however, chose to deliberately turn his back on God (I Timothy 2:14)[30]. His was an act of willful disobedience to God's instructions.

The fact that sin passes through the male of our race and not the female helps our understanding of the doctrine of the Virgin Birth.

---

[30] I Tim. 2:14 And Adam was not deceived, but the woman being deceived was in the transgression.

We are informed that our Lord Jesus Christ was born of a virgin woman (Matthew 1:23)[31]. This was a woman who had never had sexual relations with a man. The Bible also informs us that Jesus' father was the Holy Spirit, (Luke 1:34, 35;)[32], and that he was born into this world sinless (Heb 4:15)[33]. Jesus could not have been born into this world sinless if sin was transmitted through the woman of our race. Though sin filled, the woman does not pass sin from herself to another. Sin passes through the seed of the male of our race.

The virgin birth of our Lord Jesus is one of the central teachings of our Christian faith. In denying the virgin birth of Christ, one is denying the fact that he was born sinless. If Christ had been born into this world sin-filled like the rest of humanity then he would not have been an acceptable substitute for man's sin.

---

[31] Matt. 1:23 Behold, a virgin shall be with child, and shall bring forth a son, and they shall call his name Emmanuel, which being interpreted is, God with us.

[32] Luke 1:34 Then said Mary unto the angel, How shall this be, seeing I know not a man?
Luke 1:35 And the angel answered and said unto her, The Holy Ghost shall come upon thee, and the power of the Highest shall overshadow thee: therefore also that holy thing which shall be born of thee shall be called the Son of God.

[33] Heb. 4:15 For we have not an high priest which cannot be touched with the feeling of our infirmities; but was in all points tempted like as we are, yet without sin.

In their fallen, sinful state, and aware of their own nakedness, Adam and Eve attempted to cover up their sin by making their own coverings (Gen. 3:7)[34]. However, this was unacceptable to God and the Bible tells us that God intervened (Gen. 3:21)[35].

God sacrificed innocent animals to provide the means by which the first man and woman could cover their sinful state. God shed innocent blood. God knew that the shedding of innocent blood was necessary to atone for willful disobedience to his word (Heb 9:22)[36].

---

[34] Gen. 3:7 And the eyes of them both were opened, and they knew that they were naked; and they sewed fig leaves together, and made themselves aprons.

[35] Gen. 3:21 Unto Adam also and to his wife did the LORD God make coats of skins, and clothed them.

[36] Heb. 9:22 And almost all things are by the law purged with blood; and without shedding of blood is no remission.

Tainted and Stained With Sin

God's love for man didn't diminish after his fall into sin. Immediately after providing the means to cover man's sinfulness and informing Adam and Eve of the consequences of their actions, God expelled them from his garden and placed Angels with flaming swords at the entrance to bar their return (Genesis 3:24)[37]. This was done as an act of love on God's part because the Lord did not want sin filled man to return to the garden and eat of the tree of Life. To eat of the tree of Life in a sin filled state would have caused man to be forever separated from God (Genesis 3:22)[38]. God's love for man (for you and me) would not permit this to happen.

---

[37] Gen. 3:24 So he drove out the man; and he placed at the east of the garden of Eden Cherubims, and a flaming sword which turned every way, to keep the way of the tree of life.

[38] Gen. 3:22 And the LORD God said, Behold, the man is become as one of us, to know good and evil: and now, lest he put forth his hand, and take also of the tree of life, and eat, and live for ever:

The first man and woman left the garden of Eden with the faith that God would provide a way for future generations of men and women to return to fellowship with him (Genesis 3:15)[39]. As the couple stepped through the gate and departed the beautiful garden of God, they couldn't help but notice the startling transformation that had taken place on the earth. Where peace and beauty had once highlighted creation, death and decay now reigned. Animals that Adam had named and who had once played together now turned on each other in deadly combat. Plants and trees were now twisted and the air was scented with the smell of rot. Thorns and thistles sprung from the earth beneath their feet and Adam and Eve huddled in remorse aware that the whole creation was groaning because of their actions.

Satan had succeeded in regaining his control and dominion over the earth. Now he would seek to become man's god.

With Adam and Eve's failure to obey God and subsequent slid into sin, the authority and ownership God had given them over the earth was transferred to Satan. (Luke 4:6)[40]. The fallen Lucifer once more became the prince and power of the air.

---

[39] Gen. 3:15 And I will put enmity between thee and the woman, and between thy seed and her seed; it shall bruise thy head, and thou shalt bruise his heel.

[40] Luke 4:6 And the devil said unto him, All this power will I give thee, and theology of them: for that is delivered unto me; and to whomsoever I will I give it.

From his throne in the highest heavens, God the Father and his son watched as man procreated and populated the earth. Just as God had warned in his original admonition, the sin of Adam and Eve brought death upon all humanity (Romans 5:12)[41]. And Satan became successful in turning a large number of people from belief in the one true God. Sin was rampant upon the earth.

On one occasion, God visited the earth and grew disgusted with what he saw man doing (Genesis 6:5)[42]. It grieved him that he even created man and he determined that he was going to destroy all life (Genesis 6: 6,7)[43]. But God had made a promise to Adam and Eve and even in his great anger, sought out Noah and his family through whom he would preserve a remnant of the life he had made. Noah and his off spring survived the great flood and once more repopulated the earth.

---

[41] Rom. 5:12 Wherefore, as by one man sin entered into the world, and death by sin; and so death passed upon all men, for that all have sinned:

[42] Gen. 6:5 And God saw that the wickedness of man was great in the earth, and that every imagination of the thoughts of his heart was only evil continually.

[43] Gen. 6:6 And it repented the LORD that he had made man on the earth, and it grieved him at his heart.
6:7 And the LORD said, I will destroy man whom I have created from the face of the earth; both man, and beast, and the creeping thing, and the fowls of the air; for it repenteth me that I have made them.

In my heart's eye, I can imagine God returning to his throne in heaven and in the fullness of his appointed time, sending out a call across the heavenly realm. "Is anyone here," he would inquire, "who will go down and show fallen sin-filled mankind the way back to fellowship with me?" I'm sure that there would have been a hushed silence in heaven. God knew it was a very difficult thing he was asking. Who would want to give up the light and peace of heaven for the darkness and despair of a sin-filled earth? To give up the unity of harmony, peace and unity of heaven to minister among a people whose every imagination was evil continually. Yet, his great love for that people even in their fallen state was unmistakable. Heaven's inhabitants could only ponder what manner of love God the father must have for man.

Shortly, God's great love for man would be sorely tested when his only son rose from his throne and stood to his feet. "I will go, father," the pre-incarnate Jesus would have proclaimed confidently. I can imagine a gasp rushing through heaven's throng. Tears probably flowed freely as father and son would have embraced and Angels bowed low in reverence.

What manner of love is this that he, who was there in the beginning (John 1:1)[44] and by whom everything was created, (John 1:10[45]; Ephesians 3:9[46]; Hebrews 1:2)[47], he who sat upon a holy throne and shared the Godhead (Colossians 2:9)[48], he, the holy Son of God would lay down his divinity and become one of them so that he might provide the way for them to return to fellowship with the Eternal God. As realization of what was occurring would have spread through the crowd, I am sure many of heaven's throng would have stepped forward and offered to go in the Lord's stead. But all offers would have been refused. The pre-incarnate Jesus knew that this was a task that he would have to accomplish. Such was his love for his father that he would have done anything to bring him pleasure.

---

[44] John 1:1 In the beginning was the Word, and the Word was with God, and the Word was God.

[45] John 1:10 He was in the world, and the world was made by him, and the world knew him not.

[46] Eph. 3:9 And to make all men see what is the fellowship of the mystery, which from the beginning of the world hath been hid in God, who created all things by Jesus Christ:

[47] Heb. 1:2 Hath in these last days spoken unto us by his Son, whom he hath appointed heir of all things, by whom also he made the worlds;

[48] Col. 2:9 For in him dwelleth all the fullness of the Godhead bodily.

Many in heaven would have remembered how just the appearance of the Son of God in his power was sufficient to send Lucifer and his evil follower over the walls of heaven. Perhaps that's all that would be required this time as well. But that hope was dashed as they watched the Son of God remove his holy robes. They knew that this time would be different. The Son of God was laying aside his power and glory in order to become a man. He would be helpless, subject to every pain and temptation that afflicted man. The Son of God would be a human being in every sense of the word.

The Incarnate Son of God

God had promised the fallen Lucifer that someone would come to redeem mankind (Gen. 3:15)[49]. In the fullness of Gods' time, God's own son entered the world as a human infant. His mother, Mary, was a young virgin. And in obedience to the instructions of holy Angels, the Son of God was given the human name Jesus, which means, God is with us (Matt. 1:21-23)[50].

---

[49] Gen. 3:15 And I will put enmity between thee and the woman, and between thy seed and her seed; it shall bruise thy head, and thou shalt bruise his heel.

[50] Matt.1:21 And she shall bring forth a son, and thou shalt call his name JESUS: for he shall save his people from their sins.
1:22 Now all this was done, that it might be fulfilled which was spoken of the Lord by the prophet, saying,
1:23 Behold, a virgin shall be with child, and shall bring forth a son, and they shall call his name Emmanuel, which being interpreted is, God with us.

As stated earlier, Jesus' father was the third person of the Godhead, the Holy Spirit. This was necessary so that he would not have a human father and be born of the seed of man. Jesus was born of the seed of woman. This made it possible for him to be born sinless and at the same time remain a human being.

Jesus and the Fallen Lucifer

Because Jesus was born sinless, he was unlike any other human being that had ever been born. It doesn't take a great deal of imagination to understand that upon his miraculous conception and birth, Satan would have remembered God's admonition to him and gone on the offensive. For the first time since the fall of Adam and Eve a human being had entered the world who potentially could challenge his claim and authority over the earth (Luke 4:6)[51]. Everyone born up to the time of Christ's birth had been born full of sin (Romans 3:23)[52] and subject to its consequences -- death (Romans 6:23)[53]. So long as this remained humanities reality Satan would retain his earthly rule and dominion. But now someone had come who was a real threat to Satan's power.

---

[51] Luke 4:6 And the devil said unto him, All this power will I give thee, and the glory of them: for that is delivered unto me; and to whomsoever I will I give it.

[52] Rom. 3:23 For all have sinned, and come short of the glory of God;

[53] Rom. 6:23 For the wages of sin is death; but the gift of God is eternal life through Jesus Christ our Lord.

—

96

It is probable that the moment that God's son stood to his feet and proclaimed to his father that he would go and show fallen mankind the way back to fellowship, creation reverberated with the news. The news, at first, would have startled the powerful fallen Lucifer. The devil would have remembered how just the presence of the pre-incarnated Christ in his glory was sufficient to cast him from heaven. Now he was in the world, human and sinless. The Ancient of Days had warned Satan that such a one would come. Now the time had arrived.

Satan would have been delighted when he discovered that God's son had come helpless and vulnerable. The devil would have gone about the task of drawing up his battle plans in the full knowledge that the incarnate Christ had laid aside his glory and divested himself of his deity when he put on humanity. This knowledge probably spurred him on in his quest for vengeance and victory.

Satan's first attack against the incarnate Son of God came while Jesus was still an infant. Working through one of his evil servants (Herod), Satan ordered the execution of all male infants three years of age and younger in the area where it was known that Jesus had been born (Matt. 2:16)[54]. By taking the life of so many innocents, Satan demonstrated the lengths to which he would go to end the threat to his rule on the earth.

The attempt to take the life of the young deliverer was thwarted, however, when Angels warned Jesus' parents to steal away with him into the land of Egypt (Matthew 2:13)[55]. Very little is known of the childhood years of Jesus. Some insight is gained, however, when we are informed in scripture that Jesus "increased in wisdom and stature and in favor with God and man" (Luke 2:52).

---

[54] Matt. 2:16 Then Herod, when he saw that he was mocked of the wise men, was exceeding wroth, and sent forth, and slew all the children that were in Bethlehem, and in all the coasts thereof, from two years old and under, according to the time which he had diligently enquired of the wise men.

[55] Matt. 2:13 And when they were departed, behold, the angel of the Lord appeareth to Joseph in a dream, saying, Arise, and take the young child and his mother, and flee into Egypt, and be thou there until I bring thee word: for Herod will seek the young child to destroy him.

Luke 2:52 identifies for us the four areas of life with which we need to be concerned as we grow and develop. God created man for growth and by modeling Jesus we understand that that growth has to occur in the realm of the mental (wisdom) and in the realm of the physical (stature). We also need to grow spiritually (favor with God) and socially (favor with man). This same construction can be found repeated in other sections of the scriptures (see Romans 12:1,2)[56]. If, as we grow, one of these areas is lacking or overemphasized, we stand the risk of being unbalanced in our development. This should be avoided.

A further glimpse, into the spiritual zeal of Jesus, can be observed by studying Psalms 69. Beginning at verse six[57] we are given the picture of a contrite Jesus who is very zealous and desires nothing more than not to be a disappointment to God. His life is accented by fasting and by prayer. For these activities Jesus bore the reproach of his family and community. Each of us would do well to count the cost of our professed walk with God. I believe we would all come up short when measured against that which Jesus was made to endure for his faith walk.

---

[56] Rom. 12:1 I beseech you therefore, brethren, by the mercies of God, that ye present your bodies a living sacrifice, holy, acceptable unto God, which is your reasonable service.
12:2 And be not conformed to this world: but be ye transformed by the renewing of your mind, that ye may prove what is that good, and acceptable, and perfect, will of God.

[57] Ps. 69:6 Let not them that wait on thee, O Lord GOD of hosts, be ashamed for my sake: let not those that seek thee be confounded for my sake, O God of Israel.

Jesus began his public ministry at age thirty. There was no great fanfare announcing his arrival at the riverbank where his cousin, John the Baptist, called sin-filled people to repent. There was no crowd to applaud Jesus even though he had already performed at least one miracle at the wedding feast in Cana. Probably through a God-directed insight, John recognized Jesus as the perfect, sinless, man that God would use to restore his broken relationship with humankind. For that reason, John hesitated to baptize Jesus in the water. Both John and Jesus knew that water baptism was only a symbolic picture of the cleansing that takes place when a sinful person is cleansed by shed innocent blood. Jesus chose this symbolic cleansing and encouraged his cousin to proceed with the admonition, "suffer it to be so, that all righteousness might be fulfilled" (Matt. 3:15). The Lord's intent was clear, by allowing himself to be baptized, Jesus was seeking to identify with those of the human race who heeded John's call to repentance. Additionally, as Jesus stepped into the water, he symbolically took the place of all of us who sin. By being immersed beneath the water, he symbolically carried those sins into death. In rising from the watery grave, Jesus pictured those cleansed from their sins and raised in newness of life.

It was not evident that those present knew what had taken place but John knew. God had earlier told him that the one on whom he saw his Spirit descend was the one who would take away the sins of the world. When the Holy Spirit, in the form of a dove, descended on Jesus, John knew that his own ministry of preparing the way for the savior of mankind was about to end. God's son was about to begin his ministry.

Satan's Power Broken

Immediately after Jesus was baptized and anointed by God for his ministry, he was moved by the Holy Spirit to retreat into the wilderness (Mark 1:12)[58]. In this desert wilderness, Jesus would fast and pray for forty days and nights, all the while being tempted by Satan (Mark 1:13)[59]. This was probably not the first time Satan tired to tempt Jesus, we are told that Christ was tempted in every area of life that you and I are tempted in. After fasting for forty days and nights, when Jesus was near death, Satan launched his most subtle attacks. His quest was to get Jesus to do anything outside of the will of God the Father. "If thou be the Son of God," Satan would query, "then command this stone that it be made bread. (Luke 4:3). Satan knew that the fact that Jesus had not eaten was taking a toll on him. His appeal was to the natural hunger pains gnawing at the Lord's stomach. It was within Jesus' power to turn the stone to bread and eat but he knew that to do so would not have been of God. Jesus countered Satan with scripture and let the Devil know that even at the point of physical death, he was more interested in being faithful to do God's will and to wait on God to take care of his needs (John 4:31–34)[60].

---

[58] Mk. 1:12 And immediately the spirit driveth him into the wilderness.

[59] Mk. 1:13 And he was there in the wilderness forty days, tempted of Satan; and was with the wild beasts; and the angels ministered unto him.

The Kingdom's of the Earth

Next, Satan offered Jesus all the kingdoms of the world (Luke 4:5,6)[61]. A study of biblical numerology tells us that four represents the world and its systems and suggests that what Satan offered the Lord was the four systems of the world (political system, economic system, social system and religious system). These kingdoms became Satan's when he succeeded in causing man to sin. Jesus did not challenge Satan's ownership of these kingdoms as he again refused the temptation with the help of scripture. Satan would later use his kingdoms, in the person of Pilate (political), Judas (economic), the Jewish crowd (social) and the religious leaders (religious) in seeking the life of Jesus.

---

[60] Jn. 4:31 In the mean while his disciples prayed him, saying, Master, eat.
Jn. 4:32 But he said unto them, I have meat to eat that ye know not of.
4:33 Therefore said the disciples one to another, Hath any man brought him ought to eat?
Jn. 4:34 Jesus saith unto them, My meat is to do the will of him that sent me, and to finish his work.

[61] Lk. 4:5 And the devil, taking him up into an high mountain, shewed unt him all the kingdoms of the world in a moment of time.
Lk. 4:6 And the devil said unto him, All this power will I give thee, and the glory of them: for that is delivered unto me; and to whomsoever I will I give it.

After his failure to entice Jesus to turn the stone into bread, or accept the lordship of the kingdoms of the world, Satan encouraged him to prove he was God's son by attempting suicide. Jesus was to hurl himself from the pinnacle of the Temple and challenge God to send Angels to save him (Luke 4:9-11)[62]. Again Jesus refused by answering the devil's temptation with the Holy Word of God. With this final rebuff, Satan ended the temptations, but only for a short while. Jesus was the subject of Satan's attacks throughout his earthly life. Satan knew Jesus posed the greatest menace to him and his authority. He would not be content until he had disposed of his threat.

---

[62] Lk. 4:9 And he brought him to Jerusalem, and set him on a pinnacle of the temple, and said unto him, If thou be the Son of God, cast thyself down from hence:
4:10 For it is written, He shall give his angels charge over thee, to keep thee:
4:11 And in their hands they shall bear thee up, lest at any time thou dash thy foot against a stone.

It is likely that from the time Jesus was a small child, Satan worked to tempt him to do something of his own volition -- outside of the will of God. Over thirty years of trying unsuccessfully to get Jesus to sin probably left Satan frustrated and angry. Had it been possible, Satan would have avoided the wilderness temptation. He is after-all a coward and had not been successful throughout the life of Jesus. Even waiting until Jesus was near death from starvation to tempt him had proven unsuccessful. It was in his frustration over the defeat in the wilderness that Satan entertained the notion to kill Jesus. If he could remove the Christ from the world, then the threat to his rule would be ended.

Only after that season of temptations was over were Angels permitted to minister to Jesus. With their assistance he was restored to health and left the desert to begin his work of mending the relationship between God and man.

Behold – the Lamb of God

Jesus lived a model life while on earth. Luke the physician tells us that of all the things that Jesus could have done with the authority and power he received from the Holy Spirit, he chose to *walk about doing good.* (Acts 10:38)[63]. Jesus' living was not according to the standards set by man, but he lived by the higher, more perfect standard of God. Man has consistently demonstrated that he does not have the ability to keep God's commands. We murder, we cheat, we tell lies. We imagine things that are repulsive to a righteous Holy God. Jesus lived his life among us to show us by his example how to live a life marked by its love for God and for one another.

---

[63] Acts 10:38 How God anointed Jesus of Nazareth with the Holy Ghost and with power: who went about doing good, and healing all that were oppressed of the devil; for God was with him.

As the perfect Son of God, Jesus could have been anything he wanted. Satan understood this and offered him his own evil kingdom. Jesus refused his offer and during his earthly life demonstrated his mastery over sickness and disease, over nature, over the realm of the demonic and even over death itself. It is note worthy that Jesus rejected Satan's kingdom and chose instead to go about doing good. One of the Gospel writers tells us that Jesus was so full of virtue that it radiated from him like an unseen balm (Luke 8:46)[64]. The message for us in unmistakable, our lives should be crowned with going good for others. We don't need to misuse any other human being. We don't need to seek to acquire anything that belongs to someone else. We don't need to hurt or kill. We only need to do good. Any of us can do that. And we can do it for just about anyone. Doing good doesn't require wealth, nor does it require great intelligence. Doing good does not require special training it only requires a willing heart and a desire to place the well being of others above your own well being. Just do good.

---

[64] Lk. 8:46 And Jesus said, Somebody hath touched me: for I perceive that virtue is gone out of me.

Jesus Calls His Disciples

Early in his ministry, Jesus gathered to himself a group of men who would become the objects of his instruction and training. These twelve men came from different occupations and various social positions. What united them was the man, Jesus Christ. Contrary to the tradition of his day, Jesus sought these men out and called them to follow him (Mark 1:17)[65]. Then for three years he poured his life into them. These men lived with Jesus, observed him and even tried to emulate the things he did. Jesus loved these men and through them showed us how much he loved us (John 17:20)[66].

---

[65] Mk. 1:17 And Jesus said unto them, Come ye after me, and I will make you to become fishers of men.

[66] Jn. 17:20 Neither pray I for these alone, but for them also which shall believe on me through their word;

Near the end of his ministry on earth, Jesus began to inform the twelve men that he would soon be taken from them. He wanted to prepare them for the fact that he was going to be killed. Jesus never forgot the fact that he was born into the world for the express purpose of dying for mankind. He remembered how God the father had to kill innocent animals shed their blood and cover Adam and Eve for their original sin. The blood of Jesus was to be offered in similar fashion. The shedding of his innocent blood would be the least he would be required to sacrifice in order to redeem fallen mankind and restore the broken relationship with God.

Jesus in the Garden of Gethsemane

Though Jesus knew that he would have to die to secure our pardon and restore our relationship with God this did not disturb him. What did disturb him though was what he knew would be the immediate consequence of taking our sin onto himself.

After completing a final meal with his disciples, Jesus led them to the Garden of Gethsemane where he often withdrew in order to spend quiet time with his father (Matt. 26:36)[67]. It was in this garden that the Lord gave his most profound demonstration of his love for all of us. This demonstration occurred after he conducted himself a short distance from his followers and began to earnestly entreat God to let the cup pass from him (Matt. 26:39)[68]. Jesus prayed this prayer three times but each time ended the petition with the acknowledgment that he wanted the father's will above anything else. So earnest was Jesus in his desire that the cup be passed from him that scripture informs us that his blood oozed from his pours like droplets of sweat (Luke 22:44)[69].

---

[67] Mt. 26:36 Then cometh Jesus with them unto a place called Gethsemane, and saith unto the disciples, Sit ye here, while I go and pray yonder.

[68] Mt. 26:39 And he went a little farther, and fell on his face, and prayed, saying, O my Father, if it be possible, let this cup pass from me: nevertheless not as I will, but as thou wilt.

[69] Lk. 22:44 And being in an agony he prayed more earnestly: and his sweat was as it were great drops of blood falling down to the ground.

It has been supposed that the cup that Jesus wanted to pass from him was the cup of having to die on the cross. But I don't think it was the Lord's fear of physical death that troubled him. Rather, Jesus realized that when he took on himself all of the sins of mankind, then for the first time in their eternal relationship the bond between God the Father and his Son would be severed. God would have to turn his back on the sin-filled Jesus, in the same way that it was necessary for him to turn his back on sin-filled humanity. For Jesus this separation was a fate he would have wanted to avoid if possible. But because of his great love for us, fallen humanity, God could not lift that cup from Jesus, the sacrificial lamb. To do so would have meant that you and I would have had to remain in our separated sin-filled state. For that reason, Jesus resolved to drink of the cup, deeply, so that God could restore his fellowship with mankind. Jesus had told his disciples that no one could demonstrate greater love for a person than to lay down their life for that person. In order to repair the breech that separated mankind from God, Jesus would offer not only his life but his eternal relationship with his father as well. This was the Lord's agony and his joy. Later, it would prompt the Apostle John to ask the question, "What manner of love is this?" (I John 3:1)[70].

---

[70] I John 3:1 Behold, what manner of love the Father hath bestowed upon us, that we should be called the sons of God: therefore the world knoweth us not, because it knew him not.

The Son of God Judged

Shortly after his travail in the garden, temple soldier arrived at Gethsemane to arrest Jesus so that he could be led before the Jewish religious authorities and falsely convicted in a mock trial. The sudden appearance of the soldiers awakened the disciples who were so weary that they slept while Jesus had agonized. But now, with the soldier's intrusion, they were all awake and standing. Jesus took command of the potentially

volatile situation by asking the men "whom seek ye?" (John 18:4)[71] They responded that they had come for Jesus of Nazareth. To this the Lord replied, "I am" (John 18:5, 6)[72]. The Lord identifying himself in this fashion was so filled with power that the men fell backward to the ground.

---

[71] John 18:4 Jesus therefore, knowing all things that should come upon him, went forth, and said unto them, Whom seek ye?

[72] John 18:5 They answered him, Jesus of Nazareth. Jesus saith unto them, I am he. And Judas also, which betrayed him, stood with them.
18:6 As soon then as he had said unto them, I am he, they went backward, and fell to the ground.

One other time God had revealed himself to man in this fashion. Exodus tells us that in response to Moses question "who shall I say has sent me?" God instructed him to say "I am has sent me " (Exodus 3:14)[73]. When you stop to think about it, there is no better or more effective name by which to appreciate God. He is because He has always been and will always be. His name is "I am" and there is no other like him. He is the self-existent one. On this basis alone, God is worthy of our worship. Add to this the great love he must feel for us to offer himself a sacrifice for the evil within each of us and we can only stand in awe and seek to repay his sacrifice with obedience. Judas did not understand this.

After the soldiers regained their feet, Judas who had shown the soldiers the way, walked over to Jesus and kissed him on the cheek. This was done to confirm to the soldiers which of the men was, in fact, Jesus.

---

[73] Ex. 3:14 And God said unto Moses, I AM THAT I AM: and he said, Thus shalt thou say unto the children of Israel, I AM hath sent me unto you.

113

After Judas's betrayal, the soldiers bound Jesus and lead him into Jerusalem to be questioned by the Jewish religious leadership. Jesus knew that this was Satan's hour and it was for this time that he had been born into the world (John 18:37)[74]. Isaiah tells us that just as a lamb is silent before her slayers so Jesus spoke not a single word before the Jewish religious leadership (Isaiah 53:7)[75]. That is, he remained silent before them until Caiphas, the High Priest, petitioned him to answer their inquires by appealing to God the father. "I adjure you by the living God, to tell us if you be the Son of the Most High" (Matt. 26:63). Because Jesus always honors his father, he spoke but only enough to indicate clearly for them that he was the Son of God. "It is as you have said" (Matt. 27:11). With this, the High Priest tore his robes and declared that Jesus had committed blasphemy. In early Jewish society, blasphemy was a crime punishable by death. However, because the Jews were under the domination of Rome and subject to its laws, they could not order a death sentence for the Lord. It was for that reason the Jewish leadership ordered that Jesus be taken before the Roman governor, Pontius Pilate. Pilate was a politician. He understood the position of the Jewish religious

---

[74] John 18:37 Pilate therefore said unto him, Art thou a king then? Jesus answered, Thou sayest that I am a king. To this end was I born, and for this cause came I into the world, that I should bear witness unto the truth. Every one that is of the truth heareth my voice.

[75] Is. 53:7 He was oppressed, and he was afflicted, yet he opened not his mouth: he is brought as a lamb to the slaughter, and as a sheep before her shearers is dumb, so he openeth not his mouth.

leadership and he understood the authority he represented as the Roman overseer for the providence of Judea. The Jews could do nothing without his sanction, and the cost to_them for his approval would be nothing less than sworn allegiance to the Emperor of Rome. The Roman Emperors fashioned themselves to be gods. In swearing allegiance to Caesar, the Jewish leadership, in effect, turned its back on the true God and exchanged Him for a false one. Pilate used the authority of Rome and condemned Jesus Christ to death.

The Son of God Condemned

It is hard to fathom that someone could be born for the express purpose of dying. But that is exactly what Jesus Christ came to earth to do. He knew from his very beginning that he was to be God's sacrifice for the sins of mankind.

The Roman form of capital punishment was crucifixion. People were hung upon a cross until they could no longer force air into their lungs. In time, they suffocated. The death was long and agonizing. In some instances, those condemned to this type of death would linger in a state between life and death for days. Pilate and the Jewish populace of his time condemned Jesus to be crucified (John 19: 15,16)[76]. Jesus was made to carry the instrument of his own death, his cross, through the streets of Jerusalem until he fell beneath its weight. At that point a black man was pulled from the crowd and made to carry the cross the remainder of the way to a hill called Calvary (Luke 15: 21,22)[77].

---

[76] John 19:15 But they cried out, Away with him, away with him, crucify him. Pilate saith unto them, Shall I crucify your King? The chief priests answered, We have no king but Caesar.
John 19:16 Then delivered he him therefore unto them to be crucified. And they took Jesus, and led him away.

[77] Lk. 15:21 And they compel one Simon a Cyrenian, who passed by, coming out of the country, the father of Alexander and Rufus, to bear his cross.
15:22 And they bring him unto the place Golgotha, which is, being interpreted, The place of a skull.

At Calvary, Jesus was stripped of his clothing, nailed to the boards of the cross and hung between two thieves. As Jesus hung there between heaven and earth, he fulfilled his purpose for coming to earth and took on to himself sin. The perfect Son of God who had never known any type of disobedience to his father, for the first time in his life, suddenly found himself filled with the sins of humanity. As a consequence, Jesus also found his communion with God cut off. Heaven closed its doors to him and he could no longer hear the angels singing or observe his father's face. God had turned his back on him and Jesus cried out in anguish (Matt. 27: 46)[78]. This was the terrible reality that Jesus sought to avoid in the garden of Gethsemane. Yet, it was the price He was willing to pay in order to secure our pardon from God.

---

[78] Mt. 27:46 And about the ninth hour Jesus cried with a loud voice, saying, Eli, Eli, lama sabachthani? that is to say, My God, my God, why hast thou forsaken me?

With the sins of the world now firmly on Him, the moment Jesus had dreaded arrived. He was no longer in fellowship with his father. He, who throughout His life had known no sin, had become sin for us. The gospel writers tell us that as Jesus hung upon the Cross darkness covered the earth (Matt. 27:45)[79]. It was as though nature was trying to hide its face in shame. This darkness hung over the earth for about three hours and lifted when Jesus, knowing that His work on earth was finished, dismissed His spirit and permitted death to claim Him (Matt. 27:50)[80]. Death belongs to the domain of sin. So the fact that Jesus could die is one of the greatest evidences that He did, in fact, take upon himself our sins.

---

[79] Mt. 27:45 Now from the sixth hour there was darkness over all the land unto the ninth hour.

[80] Mt. 27:50 Jesus, when he had cried again with a loud voice, yielded up the ghost.

Jesus descended into Hell with our sins (Eph. 4:9,10)[81]. There, it is easy to surmise, he suffered the anguish and torment that comes with separation from God along with all of the others who had died in their sins or been banished from God's presence. Because of his great love for you and me, Jesus would have spent his eternity in Hell, separated from his heavenly father. He had come to earth to die for our sins and suffer sins consequences, so his abode in Hell was not unexpected. God hates sin and while Jesus was made sin for us, God poured out his anger and wrath against it. The terrible fury that Jesus must have had to endure we can only imagine. We know that it is a terrible thing to fall into the hands of an angry God. Jesus willingly accepted God's bitterness and anger so that we would never have to know it first hand. No one knows why Jesus would love us so much that he would endure Hell itself for us. But he did endure it and we can only thank him and love him for it. While Jesus would have spent his eternity in Hell for our benefit, Jesus knew his father and his father's great love for him. He was not surprised, therefore, when after three days in Hell, satisfying his father's anger against sin, God's love would cause him to reach into Hell and raise his only Son from among the dead (Rom. 6:4[82]; 8:11[83]).

---

[81] Eph. 4:9 (Now that he ascended, what is it but that he also descended first into the lower parts of the earth?
Eph. 4:10 He that descended is the same also that ascended up far above all heavens, that he might fill all things.)

[82] Rom. 6:4 Therefore we are buried with him by baptism into death: that like as Christ was raised up from the dead by the glory of the Father, even so we also should walk in newness of life.

God in his righteousness could not bear to look upon sin. Any sin was to be punished, even if this sin was on the person of his Son, Jesus Christ. However, God's justice could not permit an innocent to suffer. This was the divine paradox that God knew he would one day have to resolve. So, once God's wrath against sin had been fully satisfied, He looked into Hell and saw an innocent Jesus, one who had never personally sinned, enduring the anguish of divine wrath in Hell. God in his compassion raised Jesus from the dead and instead of just making him a living being as he did with Adam, he made him into a "quickening spirit" (Rom. 8:11)[84]. As a quickening spirit, Jesus became the first of his type to return from the dead. Now, through him, each of us can inherit a new life, a new beginning with God. This is the great victory of Calvary. Through Jesus Christ, we have the forgiveness of our sins and a new beginning with God the father. This is the "good news" that each of our sin sick souls longs to hear, this is the "good news" that we are privileged to share with one another. Anyone accepting Jesus Christ as personal savior is accepted, by God as a adopted child (Rom.

---

[83] Rom. 8:11 But if the Spirit of him that raised up Jesus from the dead dwell in you, he that raised up Christ from the dead shall also quicken your mortal bodies by his Spirit that dwelleth in you.

[84] Rom. 8:11 But if the Spirit of him that raised up Jesus from the dead dwell in you, he that raised up Christ from the dead shall also quicken your mortal bodies by his Spirit that dwelleth in you.

8:16,17)[85]. He welcomes us into his Holy family and permits us to sit at his table as a newly found son or daughter.

As a quickening spirit, Jesus became the first fruit of many fruits (Rom. 8:29)[86]. He became the progenitor of a new people. A people no longer ensnared by the sins of this world, a people who no longer belong to Satan. In accomplishing our freedom at Calvary, Jesus broke the power of Satan. No longer do we need to live lives in opposition to God. Our fellowship with him has been restored. Now we are free to experience life the way that He always intended. Lips that were once inclined to lie, can now pronounce blessing, a heart once given to doing wrong, can now be a well of love springing forth waters of healing. Death no longer has fear for those who are in Jesus Christ and life, itself, is now filled with anticipation and hope. Anyone in Christ is free. Life can now be abundant and full. We have been made alive to God and dead to sin. This is the bounty Jesus secured for those who embrace him.

---

[85] Rom. 8:16 The Spirit itself beareth witness with our spirit, that we are the children of God:
8:17 And if children, then heirs; heirs of God, and joint-heirs with Christ; if so be that we suffer with him, that we may be also glorified together.

[86] Rom. 8:29 For whom he did foreknow, he also did predestinate to be conformed to the image of his Son, that he might be the firstborn among many brethren.

The Birth of His Church

The crucifixion of Christ was the most pivotal event in the history of mankind. Perhaps it was the most pivotal event in all of creation. God came to earth and took on himself the form of a human being. He laid aside everything that would give him an unfair advantage and lived life like any one of us. Scripture records for us that he was tempted in every way you and I are tempted but with one difference, he never gave into the temptations (Heb. 4:15)[87]. His life was the perfect life. As a reward for living the perfect life, man hung God on a cross until he was dead.

---

[87] Heb. 4:15 For we have not an high priest which cannot be touched with the feeling of our infirmities; but was in all points tempted like as we are, yet without sin.

Why Jesus Christ had to Die

To confirm the fact that Jesus was dead, one of the Roman soldiers took his spear and thrust it through the Lord's side. The tip of the spear pierced the Lord between the ribs and punctured his heart (John 19:34)[88]. Scriptures record that when this occurred, both water and blood flowed from the wound. The Church, or the bride of Christ, was born of that water and blood that flowed freely down his side. Christ died on Calvary so that he could redeem his bride--the Church. It is not improbable that God the Father always intended that his beloved son would have a wife. The writer of Ephesians (Eph. 1:4)[89] suggests for us that before the foundation of the world was laid, God had this purpose in mind.

---

[88] Jn. 19:34 But one of the soldiers with a spear pierced his side, and forthwith came there out blood and water.

[89] Eph. 1:4 According as he hath chosen us in him before the foundation of the world, that we should be holy and without blame before him in love:

Jesus Christ accomplished this on Calvary's tree. As God's sacrificial lamb for the sins of mankind, he poured out his blood. It is through the acceptance of this love offering that man's broken relationship with God is restored. God the Father accepts all of those who accept his son's willing sacrifice as members of his own household (Rom. 8:16,17)[90]. It is then through this relationship as Christ's bride that man is elevated even above the Angels of heaven.

A Wedding, Mansion, and a Throne

Today, Jesus Christ is in heaven working to prepare that place for his beloved bride. Mansions are being built, a throne is being prepared and a wedding feast is in preparation. When all of the preparations are compete, Christ has promised that he will come again and retrieve her to himself. When this occurs, all who belong to him will be with him forever.

---

[90] Rom. 8:16 The Spirit itself beareth witness with our spirit, that we are the children of God:
8:17 And if children, then heirs; heirs of God, and joint-heirs with Christ; if so be that we suffer with him, that we may be also glorified together.

This then is the destiny of all who acknowledge their sinful condition and accept the pardon for their sin that is available only through the shed blood of Jesus Christ (Acts 4:12)[91]. Creation can only wonder at the love God must posses for man that he would take a hand full of dirt, impart his own life into it and elevate it to a throne above all other creatures. Mind cannot fathom the depth of such love. But an attempt to respond to that love can be made simply by embracing it and allowing it to use you to reach others.

This is the story of God's love for us as I understand it. It is not a complicated story, God had it committed to paper (I John 5:11,12)[92] so that man would not have an excuse when he stands before him to give an account of his life. God is a merciful God who desires that no one should perish but that all should come to repentance. The only question that needs to be decided is this, what will you do with Jesus Christ.

---

[91] Acts 4:12 Neither is there salvation in any other: for there is none other name under heaven given among men, whereby we must be saved.

[92] I John 5:11 And this is the record, that God hath given to us eternal life, and this life is in his Son.
5:12 He that hath the Son hath life; and he that hath not the Son of God hath not life.

"Calvary and its cross is the pivotal event in human history"

Part Four: The Via Delarosa

For Christians, Calvary and its cross is the pivotal event in human history. There, good triumphed over evil, the Black race was singled out for a special blessing and anointing, humanity was provided a means to reconcile with one another, and the way to peace with God was established.

After three years of public ministry, Jesus Christ was taken by the religious rulers of his time to stand trial for the crime of blasphemy. His "blasphemy" was claiming to be God on earth. Because the Jewish leadership was not permitted by the Roman authorities to sentence anyone to death, the Jewish leadership took Jesus before the Roman authorities that consented with them to put Jesus to death.

The form of capital punishment in the Roman Empire was slow death by crucifixion. Jesus was to be hung upon a cross until he suffocated. Before this was to occur, however, it was the custom of the Roman legion to exact its own punishment on offenders to the peace of the empire. The soldiers to whom Jesus was handed beat him, scourged him, spit upon him and pulled out the hairs of his beard by the handful. Then, when the sentence of death was pronounced upon him, he was forced to carry his own cross -- the instrument of his death -- upon his back to the place of execution.

The ordeal that Jesus endured at the hands of the Roman guards took its toll upon him physically and weakened him. So, as he made his way through the streets of Jerusalem carrying his cross upon his back, tradition holds that Jesus fell beneath its load on several occasions. It should not be assumed that it was only the Lord's weakened physical state that caused him to stumble and fall that fateful day. Rather, his journey was an exclamation point concerning his time on earth and served as a loud statement of love to the nations.

The Lord's love manifested itself through the dogged and anguished determination with which he bore his cross towards Calvary. Though falling beneath the load repeatedly, he did not permit the load to conquer him but continued to rise against the weight in defiance and victory.

The mystical view of race asserts that the nations of the earth were formed by the descendents of Noah's three sons, Shem, Japheth and Ham. Further, scriptures suggest that every nation will have an opportunity to stand before the Lord Jesus Christ, as the King of Kings, and declare what it has done with the responsibility of proclaiming the good news of his kingdom. Jesus knew that his sacrificial death would be the means that God would use to heal the rift that sin had made between him and mankind. He also knew that God would strengthen him physically for the rigors that his final trek along the Via Delarosa would demand. It is easy to imagine then, that as he walked along bearing his cross upon his shoulders he would have looked into the future to see what would be done with the Good News of his coming to earth. What he saw added to the weight of the burden he bore on his back and he collapsed before each of Noah's son.

Bearing the Cross for the Sons of Shem

History has already recorded the fact that when the sons of Shem (said to be the father of the Jewish nation) had the privilege and responsibility of sharing God's good news, they tried to keep it Jewish. This is the message of Jonah, the Jewish prophet whom God caused to be swallowed by a fish for three days before he would preach repentance to a Gentile nation. Before God was finished with Jonah, the prophet would request that his life be taken rather than see God show mercy to a non-Jewish people.

In the end, Jonah did preach, the city did repent and God did show his mercy. But Jonah's attitude with regard to sharing God's good news was reflective of most of Abraham's descendents. They were God's chosen people and thought the good news should only be for them. It is easy to conceive then, that the first time Jesus fell beneath Calvary's Cross was before the descendants of Shem. He fell as a rebuke for what they would do with the good news after his departure. As he carried the Cross, Jesus would have looked into the future and known in his heart that they would not be faithful to share the good news of his coming, death and resurrection. The Jews did not believe that Jesus was God's son and their savior. Those who did believe would seek to keep the good news Jewish and deny it to the rest of mankind. It would take the ministry of the Apostle Paul to remove this mantle from them and transfer it to the sons of Japheth. Jesus fell beneath the load of their selfish sin on his back.

Bearing the Cross for the Sons of Japheth

Though tired, weary, bloodied and broken, Jesus somehow found the strength to lift himself and his cross and continue his journey along the "way of sorrows" to Calvary. However, he had not struggled very far before he fell once more. This time he fell as a rebuke before the descendants of Japheth. Again, as he walked along, he would have looked into the future and seen how these people, a white people, would fill the whole world with a gospel but their "good news" would be tainted.

Before they were finished, the descendents of Japheth would try and whitewash the Word of God itself. God would become a white man and everyone of significance in the scriptures would share white skin. These notions would lead the white race to believe it self to be superior to the other nations that inhabit the planet and the recipient of a special mandate from God. Though this people would be successful in proclaiming the gospel of Christ across the world, this would be a tainted message and an evil racism would attend it and infect most of humanity. The Lord fell beneath this load. However, Jesus would lift himself and his burden a second time and continue his trek along Calvary's way.

Simeon Beneath the Cross

Finally, he would fall before the descendants of Ham and not rise without assistance. As the Lord walked along towards a fore ordained fate, he once more would have looked into the future and this time he would have seen the tremendous burden that all blacks (the descendants of Ham) would be made to bear because of nothing more than the color of their skin. This time instead of lifting the Cross and proceeding on to Golgotha alone, Christ would reach out to the Black race in a godly display of compassion. The Son of God in his suffering would accord an honor and privilege to the black man that no other people could claim. Jesus would permit a black man to take the burden of the cross from his weakened body and carry it for him in his hour of greatest need. Through Simeon the Cyrenian, the Black race would share the Lord's passion and thereby be fortified and blessed against future suffering that the Lord knew was to come.

Shortly after my conversion I was given an opportunity to watch *The Greatest Story Ever Told*. I knew next to nothing about the Bible or the context in which it was written so watching that movie helped me to understand the world that Jesus lived and ministered in. For the first time in my young Christian life I got to see Roman soldiers wearing breastplates and helmets. I understood the significance of having loins girded up and the power of the sword. As I watched, though, everyone in the movie was white until it got towards the end. As Jesus struggled down the road to Calvary a black man – Sidney Poitier – was pulled from the crowd to lift the cross from Jesus. I wouldn't understand the significance of that occurrence for my own faith walk until much later in my Christian journey.

A few months into my new Christian life I asked my white spiritual family what the Bible taught about me, and my people. Their eyes filled with tears and they reluctantly turned me to the ninth chapter of Genesis and shared with me the Curse of Ham.

They must have seen the disappointment on my young face as I hung on their words. There was no mistaking the hurt I saw in their eyes. No matter how much love existed between us, however, I knew that I could not reconcile myself to the fact that I was supposed to be forever subservient to them because of the color of my skin.

The Curse of Ham

The Curse of Ham[ii] is founded upon the Old Testament passage of Genesis 9:18 - 25[93]. Ham, one of the three sons of Noah was cursed by God through Noah. This curse occurred because Ham "looked upon his father's nakedness". As the story is told, Noah, in a wine induced state of intoxication, passed out inside his tent. Ham entered the tent, unaware of Noah's state, and saw his father's nakedness. However, instead of covering Noah and shielding his nakedness, Ham left the tent and told his brothers what he had seen. The brothers, as a show of proper respect for their father, entered the tent backward with a garment between them and covered Noah. When Noah awoke and discovered what had taken place, he uttered the following, "Cursed be Canaan! The lowest of slaves will he be to his brothers" (Genesis 9:25). Noah then proceeded to pronounce blessings on his other two sons indicating that Canaan was to be servant to them. Why Noah would react in this fashion upon awakening has been the source of much speculation.

---

[93]Gen. 9:18 And the sons of Noah, that went forth of the ark, were Shem, and Ham, and Japheth: and Ham is the father of Canaan.

9:19 These are the three sons of Noah: and of them was the whole earth overspread.

9:20 And Noah began to be an husbandman, and he planted a vineyard:

9:21 And he drank of the wine, and was drunken; and he was uncovered within his tent.

9:22 And Ham, the father of Canaan, saw the nakedness of his father, and told his two brethren without.

9:23 And Shem and Japheth took a garment, and laid it upon both their shoulders, and went backward, and covered the nakedness of their father; and their faces were backward, and they saw not their father's nakedness.

Why a Curse from Noah?

Cain Hope Felder informs us that various explanations have been offered by non-blacks to explain Noah's curse. Included among them are the thoughts that Ham (1) castrated Noah; (2) sexually assaulted Noah; or (3) committed incest with his father's wife.[iii] Felder's own explanation, however, seems the more tenable. Felder offers, "in error, Ham leaves his father uncovered (according to Hebrew tradition, an act of great shamelessness and parental disrespect)". Shem and Japheth, do the proper thing and in the proper fashion. For their show of respect the two brothers receive their father's blessing.

The Curse Considered

9:24 And Noah awoke from his wine, and knew what his younger son had done unto him.
9:25 And he said, Cursed be Canaan; a servant of servants shall he be unto his brethren.

It is important to note that within the Genesis passage Noah's curse is pronounced upon Canaan and not upon Ham. Canaan is believed to be one of the sons of Ham. Carl Ellis goes so far as to suggest that Canaan actually did commit an offensive act with Noah[iv] and history does appear to confirm that the descendants of Canaan (Ham's son) were later conquered by the descendants of Shem and Japtheth and enslaved. However, Canaan was not Ham's only son. Ham's other sons are believed to be responsible for the black-skinned people who populated other portions of Africa and later, the new world.

In later years the so-called "Curse of Ham" would be used as justification for legitimizing one of the cruelest and most dehumanizing systems of forced human bondage the world has ever devised. The black Africans brought to America would be the object of that oppression. Gayraud Wilmore is speaking to the role that belief in the Curse of Ham played in the oppression of African blacks brought to America, when he observes that:

> "It was by this interpretation of the Genesis story of the origin of the world's peoples that black converts to Christianity first learned of the cause of their misery".[v]

Just prior to my conversion, painstaking efforts were made to make sure that I understood that the Bible was God's good news for all people. Was this supposed to be the good news of the gospel for me and for black people?

Something inside of me changed the day I was introduced to the so-called Curse of Ham. I couldn't reconcile the Jesus I had been learning about with the "Christian" world that I had become a part of. The message of the one and the attitude and actions of the other no longer made sense. Sadly, I didn't know how to share the confusion with anyone in my life at that time but God.

Still, I continued to walk in the Christian world that introduced me to Christ. By this time I was associated with them so completely that I had no other community to which I belonged. I grew to realize that I was accepted and held at arms length as an outsider all at the same time but they made my Christian walk relatively comfortable and after a while I was able to coast along in Christ wondering all the while how I was a part of God's "good news."

The Power of Holy Blood

Then, God helped me to understand his good news in a way I had never considered. All of us have had the annoying experience of trying to get out a stain that just did not want to respond to our effort. The cross that Jesus bore was smeared with his blood. Is there a stain more difficult to remove than blood?

The Lord's back and forehead were badly torn from the beating and the crown of thorns. Simeon, upon lifting the cross from Jesus, would have had direct contact with Jesus' blood. This blood was unlike any other. It was the blood of God. No human being can contact God's blood without being transformed by it. Simeon who had been pressed into service on behalf of humanity in general and the Black race specifically, would have gotten his fingers in that blood. Every place that blood came into contact with Simeon's skin it would have stained and every place the blood stained it would have permeated and at each place where the blood of Christ permeated, it would have begun a work of transformation - cell by cell, molecule by molecule - until Simeon would have realized that he wasn't the same anymore. With the blood stained Cross of Christ secured upon his own back, Simeon then followed Jesus through the streets of Jerusalem and to Calvary.

History has hidden from us what happened to Simeon after he carried the cross of Christ. Some scholars suggest that he became one of the pillars of the early Christian church and helped commission Paul and Barnabas for their missional outreach to the gentile peoples. I think that God left his fate intentionally obscure simply because Simeon represents every Christian who finds himself beneath the cross of Christ, smeared with the Lord's pure and holy blood. When this writer found himself kneeling beneath the cross and felt Christ's blood dripping on him, he realized that something beyond this world and reality was happening to him. When I arose from that spot, even though I nor anyone associated with me could tell it immediately, I was different. Growing into the knowledge and assurance that Christ's blood made me different when I kneeled at the foot of the Cross has caused me to seek to walk differently in this life.

I now understand that we, who are in Christ, belong to a kingdom not of this world (John 18:36)[94]. This new kingdom transcends skin colors and world systems. It transcends prejudices and hatred. This new kingdom is built upon a foundation of love and is marked by the fact within its boundaries there is no greed and there is no fear. This is the good news that God wants us to understand. Everyone who has come into contact with the blood of Christ is a new creation. As such all of the old things that bound us are passed away and everything has become brand new (II Corinthians 5:17)[95].

---

[94] Jn. 18:36 Jesus answered, My kingdom is not of this world: if my kingdom were of this world, then would my servants fight, that I should not be delivered to the Jews: but now is my kingdom not from hence.

[95] II Cor. 5:17 Therefore if any man be in Christ, he is a new creature: old things are passed away; behold, all things are become new.

Now our heart's desire is to be found worthy of the Lord Jesus Christ and his sacrifice for us so that we can share a place in his kingdom. None should seek to keep Christ hanging on the Cross dying all over again for our sin. And when we finally stand before him to give an account of our lives, we should seek to stand before him with pure hearts. John Wesley would say that we are on a quest in this world to live lives crowned with personal holiness walking in communities of Grace. Christ, through his Holy Spirit, walks this journey through life with us and that knowledge should give us great joy. For the Holy Spirit's work is to grow us into the very bride of Christ. We are being transformed and when that transformation is complete we will be nothing less than the *glory of the Lord*.

The Glory of the Lord

"Father, return to me the glory we shared . . ." this request from Christ is part of the beginning petition of John 17, a passage rightly understood as the Lord's prayer. I had always assumed that Christ was asking his father to let him shine once again with the brightness of heaven and once more be seen in all of his royalty. But as I've studied this prayer I am coming to realize that the Lord's request is much deeper than that. In verse 10[96] of this chapter, Christ explains that we who believe in him and who are being transformed by his blood and his word are his glory. Christ shines in and through us. When any of his creation looks on us, they will see Christ's handiwork being reflected from us and praise him.

In John 17:24[97] the Lord asks his father to permit us to be with him where he is so that we can behold his glory. Not only will we be able to observe Christ's heavenly splendor, we will be able to see each other realizing that we are with him because of his sacrifice, and in viewing one another will understand that we are looking at the bodily representation of his glory in each other. Christ poured himself out into us and because of that act we will shine with him throughout eternity.

---

[96] Jn. 17:10 And all mine are thine, and thine are mine; and I am glorified in them.
[97] Jn. 17:24 Father, I will that they also, whom thou hast given me, be with me where I am; that they may behold my glory, which thou hast given me: for thou lovedst me before the foundation of the world.

I am humbled when I reflect upon the fact that throughout eternity when the rest of creation looks at us, they will be seeing nothing less than *the glory of the lord*. Such notions make me want to behave differently, while on this earth. How could we, the sons of Adam, formed, from a handful of dust, ever come to a place in our development where we would be the Lord's glory? It is in wrestling with that question that the full impact of God's love for us is revealed and understood. It is here that the hidden trove of God's treasure lies. Hidden only from those who would seek to acquire it through improper means. Hidden only from those who have impure motives and unclean hearts. God's treasure is not buried but sits openly upon the face of the earth. Nor is there a limit to the amount that one can appropriate to him or her self. God's wealth is limitless. All that is required of us is a personal, honest relationship with Jesus Christ, God's son and an eager quest to discover God's treasure.

"I was certain that they had misquoted the verse"

Part Five: The Giving of Gifts

In Ephesians 4:8-12[98], the Apostle Paul paints a wonderful picture of the resurrected Christ ascending from the grave and dispensing gifts (treasure) to mankind as he rises through the heavens. These gifts are given to believers and were to be used for the building up of God's kingdom on earth. In painting this picture, Paul was drawing from a passage in Psalms chapter 68. Recently, I worked with a group of pastors who, in the production of a final research paper, sought to make their point by quoting from the Psalms 68 passage. However, they quoted verse 18 as saying "and men gave gifts to Him." I was certain that they had misquoted the verse until I looked it up in an NIV version of the Bible[99]. They were correct. The verse stated that as Christ was ascending after his resurrection men gave gifts to him. This realization caused me to ponder just exactly what type of gifts the risen savior of humankind would seek to receive from men?

---

[98] Eph. 4:8 Wherefore he saith, When he ascended up on high, he led captivity captive, and gave gifts unto men.
4:9 (Now that he ascended, what is it but that he also descended first into the lower parts of the earth?
4:10 He that descended is the same also that ascended up far above all heavens, that he might fill all things.)
4:11 And he gave some, apostles; and some, prophets; and some, evangelists; and some, pastors and teachers;
4:12 For the perfecting of the saints, for the work of the ministry, for the edifying of the body of Christ:

[99] Ps. 68:18 When you ascended on high, you led captives in your train; you received gifts from men, even from [Or gifts for men, even] the rebellious — that you, [Or they] O LORD God, might dwell there.

Gifts for the Risen Christ

I knew from Sunday school lessons and countless retellings of the Christmas story that at the birth of the King of Kings wise men brought him gifts of gold, frankincense and myrrh. These were all very valuable items that were befitting a king. However, Jesus, as the risen Lord had no need for material valuables. Still, in the spirit of Harold Grouse we try to give Christ our best.

In 1902, Harold Grouse advised everyone to "Give of your best to the Master". He probably had Proverbs 3:9 in mind as he wrote. Proverbs 3:9, counsels "Honor the LORD with your possessions, And with the first-fruits of all your increase." So we tithe, and share our possessions as much as we are able. Seeking to give God our very best. There is nothing wrong with this. God is pleased when we share in this fashion. However, I'm not sure that these are the gifts that a resurrected savior would want to see those who belong to him offering. God the Father had already bestowed upon the risen Christ all power and authority. Given that fact, what kind of gifts could man give to the risen Lord of eternity that would please him?

While reflecting on this question the Holy Spirit spoke to my heart and reminded me of the seasons of growth through which I had passed as he has worked with me in the course of my journey. With his guidance it started to become apparent that the gifts that Christ seeks from those of us who have embraced him as our Lord and savior include things like our lust, envy, bitterness, greed, and hate to name a few. The risen Christ would have gladly received our prejudice, our bigotry and malice. He would happily take our insecurities and failures. The gifts the risen Christ desires from us are all of those things deep inside of us that keep us separated from himself and his Holy Father. He died in order to give us life and to remove from us those things that would have kept us bound to death and the grave.

Gifts from the Risen Christ

In exchange for those "gifts" from man, Christ gives gifts. The Lord's gifts include peace, joy, longsuffering, temperance, meekness, gentleness, faith and love. The fact that Christ would be willing to impart such wonderful gifts in exchange for sin's residue in us speaks to the depth of his love and allows us to peek into God's treasure trove. Jesus Christ loves us and like his father desires only good things for our present living and our future.

It tends to be difficult for us to comprehend that someone would do this for us. The difficulty comes because of the realization that we still labor under the influence of sin within. Christ on the other hand has no sin of his own to contend with. Neither is he selfish or fearful. This spirit in him is one of the greatest gifts that he extends to us. His only request in exchange for the gift of his Spirit is that we be obedient to do the things the Spirit asks of us.

His Holy Spirit

In an effort to ensure that we understood the depths of his holy love, the risen Christ dispatched his Holy Spirit to be our constant companion. It is Christ's Spirit that guides us into the knowledge of the degree to which we are growing into the gifts the Lord offers us. For that reason the Apostle Paul calls those gifts the fruit of the spirit (Gal. 5:22,23)[100] because it is the tangible proof that the Holy Spirit is at work and resides in us.

---

[100] Gal. 5:22 But the fruit of the Spirit is love, joy, peace, longsuffering, gentleness, goodness, faith,
5:23 Meekness, temperance: against such there is no law.

As Christ's Holy blood courses through us, it begins a work of transformation and as we grow in our relationship with Christ the Holy Spirit ensures that we grow into that relationship in the proper fashion. The proper fashion sees us slowly evidencing the fruit of the spirit while surrendering more and more of those things that keep us separated from a Holy God. The process is slow to ensure that the surrendering is sincere and intentional on our part.

Christ does not impose his will on us but waits for us to grow into it. Thereby allowing him to assume the lordship of our lives in a way that does not negate our individual free will. Innocence is gone and we now know the difference between right and wrong. Because of the sin within us, we often choose to do the wrong but we don't have to. Christ has given us his Spirit and ability to resist sin's influence. Each time that we do this successfully, we grow a little bit stronger in the ways of Christ and he rewards us with his peace.

Seeing the Face of God

Because of its mild, temperate climate, California tends to attract a large number of individuals who make their home on its streets. Often these people can be found clustered around those places where Christians congregate. There is an unspoken notion that Christians are easy targets for panhandlers and beggars so it tends to be a bit easier for them to get a little money for the things they consider important. One Seminary in the heart of downtown Pasadena tended to be a favorite haunt however the homeless and destitute knew to stay on the periphery of the campus otherwise they were certain to attract the attention of the campus security and that was a thing to be avoided. On one particular day however, one of the homeless decided to walk through the campus grounds and just as soon as his foot touched one of its cobblestone walks, students began to take note of his presence.

They could tell the man was homeless just from his appearance. His clothes were ragged and disheveled, his hair unkempt. His feet were shod with worn sandals and his body obviously hadn't contacted any water in quite some time. The most telling thing about the man however was the way he walked bent over while mumbling to himself. His words were unintelligible but it didn't really matter because no one wanted to get close enough to him to discern what he was saying.

As he made his way across the cobblestone walkway, muttering, pockets of students began to stop and observe him. This was an unusual occurrence for the campus and before long a sizeable crowd had gathered. The man made his way almost to the center of the campus along the cobblestone walk when he stopped and turned to face one of the institutions larger buildings. The building housed the library and the man shuffled his way up the half dozen steps to its entrance. Once inside the large double glass doors to the library the man was stopped by a large wooden barrier that had been designed to prevent a person from entering or leaving the library with books that had not been checked. His progress thus halted, the man turned towards a frail little old woman on the other side of the barrier and shouted at the top of his lungs "I want to see the face of God." This outburst startled the woman and caused everyone in the library to leave their seats and make their way to strategic locations were they could see what was causing the commotion. The woman who was very familiar with the books in the library thought quickly and was about to grab a book that contained a portrait of Christ when the man shouted a second time, "I want to see the face of God." The woman tried to smile at the man and began to direct him to the book and picture she held in her hand when the man exclaimed, "I don't want to see any picture. I want to see the face of God." Before anyone could respond further, security was upon the vagrant forcefully escorting him from the building.

The homeless man probably never realized it but he got his wish that afternoon. As he looked across that barrier at the little old woman he was looking into the face of God for him and as she stared back at him from behind the barrier, she was looking into the face of God for her. It is a lesson that should not be lost on any of us who name the name of Christ as savior. We are the bodily representation of God on earth for an often desperate and needy world. It's the Holy Spirit who convicts our hearts whenever we fail to live up to that responsibility.

The Gift of Growth

I wrestled throughout my high school years and can remember how difficult it was to learn to master the various skills associated with the sport. However constant practice, two hours per day, six day per week, eventually helped the team arrive at a proficiency level that made us the talk of Northwestern Pennsylvania. Our practices were built around two primary tasks. The first task was to teach us how to take an opponent down to the mat from a standing position.

The second task was to teach us how to rise to our feet from a base position while escaping our opponents' grasp. We were in our base position when we rested on our hands and knees, locked our joints and practiced being immovable. No matter what an opponent did to us while we were on our base we were not to be dislodged. In this way we were taught that we could avoid or escape danger. Often during a match, even with hundreds of people in the stands shouting and screaming, when we would find ourselves in some sort of difficulty, we would somehow only hear our coaches voice admonishing us, "get back to your base, get back to your base." We knew that he was telling us to get to our hands and knees, lock our joints and be immovable.

This faith in Jesus Christ is the base upon which my faith rests. From its foundation I have learned to study the scriptures and to test the lessons of life. While upon the foundation of Christ I have learned to rest on all fours, lock my joints and practice being immoveable. And I have learned like the Apostle Paul, that I am crucified with Christ; nevertheless I live; yet not I but Christ lives in me and the life which I now live in the flesh I live by the faith of the Son of God, who loved me, and gave himself for me (Galatians 2:20)[101]. Paul found both strength and joy in this acknowledgment. I have found peace. A divine peace in the midst of the struggles of this present world that helps to understand that God's riches are not reserved for heaven alone. We can partake of his bounty here and now. Andre Crouch was speaking to this truth when he penned the words "If heaven never was promised to me, neither God's promise to live eternally, It's been worth it just having the Lord in my life. I was living in a world of darkness. He came along and brought me the light."[vi]

Salvation – the greatest gift of all

Salvation is the gift of God. I've heard this phrase from my earliest Christian beginnings. Christ has saved me, is saving me and will save me. Even though I've heard this truth, I am only now beginning to understand what it means.

---

[101] Gal. 2:20 I am crucified with Christ: neverthless I live; yet not I, but Christ liveth in me: and the life which I now live in the flesh I live by the faith of the Son of God, who loved me, and gave himself for me.

I was ten years old when my parents moved me from the black part of our little community and into the white section called the 5th Ward. To get into 5th Ward one has to cross a bridge that spans French Creek. French Creek coursed through and around our Pennsylvania community and was well known for its fishing and swimming. Shortly after our family arrived at our new home, I set out to explore 5th Ward and soon ran into Jimmy, a 10 year-old local who offered to take me to a favorite neighborhood-swimming hole.

It was one of those hot, humid, Pennsylvania summer afternoons and a swim sounded like the perfect thing to do. So I agreed and fifteen minutes later Jimmy and I stood on the bank of French Creek next to a massive old Oak tree. A portion of the trees branches extended out over the water and one branch had a knotted rope fastened to it. Jimmy grabbed the rope and showed me how it was used to swing out over the water. As I watched, he let go of the rope and plunged into the water's depths. Almost immediately he surfaced, swam back to the shore and indicated that it was my turn. Filled with the excitement of finding a new friend and the carelessness of youth, I grabbed the rope, swung out over the water and let go. When my feet failed to find the bottom of the creek bed, I realized that I had made a mistake. For the first time in my life I was in water over my head and for the first time in my life, I realized that I couldn't swim.

For years my father had been taking my siblings and me to a little spot on French Creek where we could sit on the water's bed and still only have it come up to our chest. Occasionally we would flip over onto our bellies and splash in the cool water being assured all the while that we were swimming. So you can imagine my great surprise on this occasion, with Jimmy, to discover that I didn't know how to swim at all. My father had misled me and now I was in a struggle for my very life. My eyes flew open in the murky depths and I flailed at the water until I could see daylight above me. Then, suddenly my toe caught hold of something firm and gave me support so that I could push upward and get air. When I came back down, my entire foot rested on the same solid surface and with my head now above the water line, I was able to beginning to walk slowly towards the bank where Jimmy was almost in a panic.

Once close enough, Jimmy reached out his hand and pulled me the rest of the way into the shore and once he knew that I was safe, dashed out of the water and disappeared. The next day he could be seen shouting to anyone who would listen how he had saved my life. He helped but I knew that some other force was the source of my "salvation" that afternoon.

Probably because of the experience at French Creek at age ten, after my conversion, salvation was always associated with the state of being saved from some danger. Jesus came bringing salvation. Meaning that Jesus came to rescue from the danger of sin and its consequences. To accomplish this Jesus had to offer himself on our behalf thus becoming the source of our salvation. What is there about salvation that this would be necessary?

The Sinner's Prayer

With the understanding that Jesus is the source of our salvation it becomes easy to take the next step and assert that if one is interested in being free from sin and its consequences then one only needs to accept Jesus as savior. Countless millions of us have done that very thing by praying a simple prayer. The prayer goes something like this:

> Lord Jesus I know that I am a sinner and that you came to die for my sin and make me a new person. Please come into my heart and cleanse me from my sin. I want to follow and serve you.

After mouthing those words (or words similar) we are taught that Christ has entered our heart and begun a work within us to negate sin's influence and consequence. We then are free to go on living our lives in the full confidence that when we die we will be with Christ in heaven. We've been saved, once and forever. There is no force on earth that can pluck us out of his hand. We are eternally secure.

After my conversion, I was indoctrinated like this and what resulted was a notion that I could live pretty much any way that I wanted so long as I was under the radar of whatever Christian community I aligned myself with. However, in time this notion began to feel disingenuous. There was no growth in Christ and I came to feel that he continuously hung on Calvary's Cross paying the penalty for my sin. I wanted better for him and for me. I wouldn't realize it until I joined the faculty of Asbury Seminary and began studies in the life and work of John Wesley but I was on a quest for a sense of holiness that would make me responsible for my walk and my growth.

A Wesleyan Understanding

Unlike the teaching I received during my early Christian walk, those who embrace Wesleyan notions of Christianity do not believe in eternal security. Rather, they teach that an individual who has accepted Christ as personal savior needs to make an intentional and deliberate choice to live a life growing into more and more intimate levels of relationship with him. It's the relationship with the risen Christ that has the primacy. As we grow more and more intimate in our union, any desire to continue conversations, engage in activities or harbor desires that would be injurious to him and his spirit become distasteful to us. And as the love between us increases – that is as we grow into the depths of his love for us – we become more and more assured of our place with him. This means, of course, that an individual can always choose to step out of the relationship with Christ and continue on his own way. But to help insure that a believer continues along the path of growth with Christ, all believers are encouraged to become involved with a community of believers. The community helps to support our growth and development.

The Gift of God

At the beginning of this section I stated that salvation is the gift of God[102] and that is exactly what it is. What is there about salvation that Christ would have to offer himself to save us? Simply that Jesus is so beloved by his father that God looks through his son to see us. He then extends through his son his very person. In other words, salvation is obtained when God gives us himself[vii] through his son Jesus[103]. Just as his son Jesus Christ gave himself to secure our pardon, God gives himself to us as the loving father. Because of who and what he is, when God gives us himself, we are saved. Salvation is the greatest gift of all because salvation comes when God, who is life itself, gives God. This is the ultimate and the reason that Christ is so careful to examine the heart of all who come before him asserting that they've been saved. Scripture affirms that many will hear the unpleasant instruction from Christ for that individual to "depart from me ye who work iniquity for we never knew each other."

---

[102] Eph. 2:8 For by grace are ye saved through faith; and that not of yourselves: it is the gift of God:
2:9 Not of works, lest any man should boast.

[103] Acts 4:12 Neither is there salvation in any other: for there is none other name under heaven given among men, whereby we must be saved.

"Jesus deposited the "mother lode" of God's riches at the foot of his cross"

Epilogue

This journey began with a question, why am I here? The answer to that question is, I am here so that I could discover where God has placed his deep riches and in locating the storehouse of his treasures, begin a process of mining them. Of course the key to God's riches are to be found in the person and work of his son, Jesus Christ. Jesus deposited the "mother lode" of God's riches at the foot of his cross.

Jesus came to earth to show mankind that true wealth is found not in material resources but in the quality of ones character and spirit. True wealth is acquired when one so loves another that he or she is willing to lay down their life for the benefit of that other person. True wealth is found in the quality of ones life.

Such wealth is not acquired easily. It is the fruit of a relationship with Jesus Christ and an intentional surrendering to his will. This surrendering is made easier when we realize the transforming power of the Lord's holy blood and embrace what his blood did and is doing for us as we journey through this life. The secret to discovering where God's riches are hidden is to be found in contacting the spilled blood of his innocent son – Jesus Christ.

If you have not accepted Christ as your personal savior or knelt beneath his cross to meet him at that level to give him your gifts, let me encourage you to do so. It only requires a simple prayer and commitment to live your life for him instead of for yourself. In exchange Christ will give you his gifts and a personal guide (the Holy Spirit) to the treasure trove of God's greatest riches.

In discovering the source of God's riches for myself I have discovered that his riches have helped to transcend the hurt and pain of life in a sin-tainted world. He makes possible a heart that forgives. He makes possible a heart that loves.

Notes

[i] This was confirmed for me when I had an opportunity to watch the 1995 movie, *Sabrina* starring Harrison Ford and Julia Ormond.

[ii] According to Carl Ellis, President of Project Joseph (an African American US mission developed to equip the church in America to deal with the incursion of Islam into the African American community), the original formulation of the Curse of Ham was done by Muslim scholars to help justify the enslavement of Africans on the continent of Africa.

[iii] Felder, Cain Hope., *Stoney the Road We Trod.* 1991. P. 131.

[iv] Ellis, Carl., *Free At Last?* Intervarsity Press. 1996. P.25

[v] Wilmore, Gayraud. *Black Religion Black Radicalism.* 1982. P. 119

[vi] Andre Crouch. "If Heaven Never Was Promised to Me." *The Best of Andre.* Compendia Records, 1993.

[vii] Drawing from Ephesians 2:8,9 most scholars seek to contrast faith and works because of the preposition "of". However a study of the construction reveals that the form "of God" is in the Genitive case and when understood as a Genitive of Material (consisting of) then the reading that salvation consists of God giving himself is a proper and valid rendering of the text.

Recommended Resources

Billheimer, Paul, *Destined for the Throne*. Fort Washington, PA: The Christian Literature Crusade, 1987

Day, Millard F., *Basic Bible Doctrines*. Chicago: Moody Press, 1976

DeHaan, M.R. *Portraits of Christ in Genesis*. Grand Rapids: Zondervan Publishing House, 1967.

Ellis, Carl. *Free at Last*. Chicago: Intervarsity Press, 1996.

Essex, Michael. *Jesus in Genesis*. Alachua, FL: Bridge Logos Publishers, 1975.

Felder, Cain Hope., *Stoney the Road We Trod*. Minneapolis: Fortress Press, 1991.

Maeder, Gary., *The Christian Life: Issues and Answers*. Glendale, CA: G/L Regal Books, 1976

Wilmore, Gayraud. *Black Religion, Black Radicalism*. New York: Orbis Books, 1982.

Made in the USA
Middletown, DE
23 November 2020